REAL SOLUTIONS
for Living With ADHD

REAL SOLUTIONS
for Living With ADHD

John H. Timmerman

VINE
BOOKS

SERVANT PUBLICATIONS
ANN ARBOR, MICHIGAN

Vine Books is an imprint of Servant Publications especially designed to serve
evangelical Christians.

Servant Publications—Mission Statement
We are dedicated to publishing books that spread the gospel of Jesus
Christ, help Christians to live in accordance with that gospel, promote
renewal in the church, and bear witness to Christian unity.

All scripture quotations, unless indicated, are taken from the HOLY BIBLE,
NEW INTERNATIONAL VERSION. Copyright 1973, 1978, 1984 by International Bible Society. Used by permission of Zondervan Publishing House.
All rights reserved.

Although the men and women whose stories are told in this book are real,
all names have been changed to protect the privacy of those involved.

Published by Servant Publications
P.O. Box 8617
Ann Arbor, Michigan 48107
www.servantpub.com

Cover design: UDG|DesignWorks, Sisters, Oregon

02 03 04 05 10 9 8 7 6 5 4 3 2 1

Printed in the United States of America
ISBN 1-56955-304-1

Library of Congress
Cataloging in Publication Division
101 Independence Ave., S.E.
Washington, D.C. 20540-4320

Library of Congress Cataloging-in-Publication Data

Timmerman, John H.
    Real solutions for living with ADHD / John H. Timmerman.
        p. cm.
    Includes bibliographical references and index.
    ISBN 1-56955-304-1
    1. Attention-deficit hyperactivity disorder–Popular works. 2. Attention-
deficit disorder in adults–Popular works. I. Title.
    RJ506.H9 T555 2002

                                                            616.85'89–dc21

                         2002000228

For Peggy Knoll

Thanks for everything.

Contents

Acknowledgments

I especially want to thank the many people whom I interviewed during the course of researching this book. Although their names have been fictionalized, their stories are authentic. The real story always lies behind the facts and statistics, in the daily lives of people.

I also acknowledge materials reprinted with permission from the *Diagnostic and Statistical Manual of Mental Disorders*, Fourth Edition, Text Revision. Copyright 2000 by the American Psychiatric Association.

Introduction

Summertime, during the 1950s. My friends and I passed the slow, hot days of our youth playing baseball on the tar playground of the old school. By late July the ball was held together with black electrical tape foraged out of one of our garages. In the afternoon, when the tar got sticky and hot under the soles of our sneakers, someone brought out a portable radio and tuned it to the afternoon Tigers game. We lounged in the shade of the generous maples.

That little red GE portable with its D-cell batteries carried the crack of the bat clean to our little stretch of Neland Avenue, and we imagined ourselves in Detroit, or Cleveland, or at Yankee Stadium. There we were on the diamond, swinging the bat, legging it out around the bases as the crowd cheered our home runs.

For me, however, the highlight of every summer was the week I got to spend at a friend's cottage on the shores of Lake Michigan. If baseball was my fantasy, this was the dream I lived for all summer. It was an old cottage, built high on the dunes overlooking the lake. I still remember that it had 113 steps from beach to cottage. My friend and I would race each way, up and down. When the lake was calm, we swam far out, so far that the cottage seemed a pinprick atop the blazing silver sand. When the lake rumbled up its big waves, we frolicked on the dunes. Once I rolled down a dune and landed in a nest of milk snakes.

If the highlight of my summer was going to the cottage, the highlight of the week was Saturday afternoon. My friend's dad drove out for the weekends, taking me home when he returned to work Monday morning. At noon on Saturday he would check to see if all of our chores were done. We had a good-sized list: gathering wood for the fireplace, sweeping the cottage, washing the car. We worked hard, and the reward was great.

When we were done, my friend's father handed us a two-dollar roll of nickels. We then walked two miles down the country road to a quaint little store called The Country Cupboard. It was like the modern Quik-Stops, a place for people who didn't want to drive the ten miles into Holland or Grand Haven to pick up milk, bread, and other perishables. It also stocked a plentitude—a true feast—of candy, just waiting for the weekend allowances to roll in. And along one wall— the north wall, as I remember—it held a row of five pinball machines. That's where we spent Saturday afternoon.

Now, the thing about pinball, in the relatively simple machinery of that time, was that a nickel could get you a lot of playing time. And the longer you played, the better you got. The game was all about leverage and timing, knowing how firmly you could knock the edge with a knee before you got the deadly red *Tilt* sign. Game ended. To really play it well, though, you almost had to get your head inside the game. The focus took over everything. The world outside shut down. You were there—inside the game.

Years later I wondered why it was that the game kept playing inside *me*. Those snapping lights and darting balls careened inside my head, and I didn't know who was flipping the levers or kneeing me to the edge of *Tilt*.

In those years I was simply known as "restless" or "couldn't sit still." Not "bad," not "naughty," but "couldn't sit still" aplenty. In church, for example, I squirmed like a caterpillar on a hot sidewalk no matter how many peppermints my father forked my way (or the occasional pinch on the leg from my mother).

Not coming from a family of means, I received a green woolen "church suit" for my eighth birthday, several sizes too large so I could wear it until I was twelve or so, by which time my mother had let out the sleeves and cuffs to the limit. How I sweated and itched through those church services, seated in our customary pew in the back where the "restless" kids were. We didn't have any medical name for that restlessness then. We just couldn't sit still. We sweated and itched and twitched when we tried to do it.

I'm not at all certain now, looking back, how but for the grace of God I got through grade school and high school. I have sometimes said that entering junior high was like entering a dark tunnel, and I came out at the end of high school unscathed by learning anything. I know that I spent a lot of the time staring out the window, watching the weather outside and wishing with all of my heart I was "out there"—anywhere but "in here."

I do remember comments like "He has so much potential," or "If he'd only pay attention," or the clincher, "If he'd only stay out of trouble," while I sat squirming with my parents at parent-teacher conferences. But once in a while something like this would slip through: "He has so much creative talent. He's really a very bright boy. I just don't know what the trouble is."

"Bright boy!" At that age—junior high and high school—I

didn't believe it. Nor did I really care, except for those moments that would creep up on me, those rare moments when I would actually try to study but would then feel I was going mad. Why did I read a paragraph five times and still have no idea what it said? Pythagorean theorems just sat there on the page, meaningless. I might as well have been looking at Greek. (I once took a semester of Greek in college just to test myself. I learned the alphabet—and forgot it by the start of the next term.)

Somehow, though, I did make it on through college and graduate school, using speed reading (appropriate!) and a form of self-hypnosis I learned from attending seminars with my wife, a nurse in the newly burgeoning field of psychiatric nursing. Even then it struck me as terribly odd that I couldn't remember the simplest things—where I had left my car keys, how to get to a nearby town—but could at some times "hyperfocus," taking in huge amounts of information with nearly perfect recall. It was like getting my mind inside the pinball machine.

Finally, armed with a new Ph.D., I began my college teaching career. Even then the pinballs kept whirling in my brain. In some respects this served me well. In the classroom I had enough energy for ten people. Every session was a performance, scripted to the last minute. The evaluations I received were glowing. When I read them, I didn't believe them.

But after classes I'd shut my office door and collapse. The more people told me how well I did, the worse I thought I was and the more I believed I had to work harder. My self-esteem went in the wastebasket each night along with the day's accumulation of scrap paper.

The worst times were exam periods. My classes were

packed, thanks to those glowing evaluations. One semester I had 212 students. (I've learned since to keep the total under a hundred.) And because I teach literature courses, the exams were mostly essay. When I had to grade them, I found I could complete no more than one before that old pinball machine went *Tilt* again and I would have to go get a cup of coffee or go for a walk—anything. I just couldn't sit there anymore.

Then one day I found myself next to the unfinished exams, head down on my arms and weeping. A man nearing middle age, at the height of his career. Respected by his colleagues. Praised by his students. Author of textbooks and other books, plus a shelfful of articles. Head down, bawling his eyes out. Only the short-circuiting lights of the pinball machine burning redly in his head.

My wife, of course, had not been oblivious to the trouble I was having. Although she had stopped working full-time as a nurse as our four children were born, she had not lost her well-informed professional perspective. She had suggested several times that I needed specialized help. Each time I ignored her with that classic male reply, "I'll be okay," or "Don't worry, I'll make it."

What a way to be okay. What a lousy way to "make it"!

The breakthrough for us came in a most unusual way. We were having one of our children, then about four years old, evaluated by a psychologist. That's right—our child was restless, couldn't sit still, and was impulsive.

As part of the process, my wife, Pat, and I had to fill out a questionnaire for parents of children with ADHD. After completing mine, I turned to Pat and said, "I can't believe this. Every one of these applies to me."

She looked at me with a twinkle in her eye and said, "That's supposed to be an evaluation for our child, not you."

"Oh," I said, somewhat stunned. "I thought it was for me."

At first my discovery was an enormous relief. There was a name, ADHD, I could give to this thing that lived in my brain. It was no longer a hyperwired pinball machine. It was an illness other people knew about—and knew how to treat. *And I wasn't alone.*

This initial reaction is common. I'm not just weird. *I have an illness, but I am not the illness I have.* These are some of the most important words in the vocabulary of a person with ADHD.

Once I recognized that I had this illness, I knew I needed treatment for it. Although my particular case was complicated, I learned, by also having bipolar disorder, genuine treatment, with medicine and therapy, was available. (I will have something to say later about the relationship between ADHD and other disorders.)

I write these pages, then, from firsthand experience. I know, deep within, exactly what you or your loved one has been going through. I know about denial, acceptance, despair, and hope.

As I went through those stages myself (often wishing that I had known many years ago what I know now), I felt the compelling need to research this illness, to learn how it works in the human brain and in the human lives we live. What I discovered is the fact that there are indeed real solutions to living with the very real difficulties of ADHD.

Let me underscore this fact: those of us who have this illness, or have loved ones with this illness, are not just diagnostic entities. We are living with the illness, but *we are not the illness itself*—no more so than a person with a broken leg is herself a broken leg, no more so than a person with diabetes is himself diabetes, no more so than a chair with a chipped rail ceases to be a chair but becomes a chipped rail.

Finally, and always, we never cease to be children of a loving God—the same who has formed us in our mothers' wombs, who has our names engraved on the palms of his hands, and who continues to say, *You are precious in my sight.*

Those points are absolute and unarguable. Accepting them, we can begin to examine the practical solutions for living with ADHD.

ONE

Clearing Away the Myths

So many misconceptions swirl around the illness of ADHD that it is sometimes difficult to capture the reality. Think of it as looking at a mountain range on a rainy, cloudy day. Perspective diminishes. Rocks and heights appear or disappear as rain clouds sweep past. The first step toward understanding, then, is to clear the air of several of these distorting myths.

The Bad Person Myth

Primary among these myths—and one that parents might even hear from teachers—is that this child is just a "bad kid." True, his or her behavior might at times be "bad," but the child is not. It is also true that the child (or adult) might frequently feel bad because of certain actions. Because of this sense of feeling bad for actions done, particularly in children, it is not unusual for depression to plague the person with this illness.

Moreover, the idea spread in some circles that the behavior of ADHD children was simply the result of bad parenting. If children behave badly, the myth has it, then their parents must be bad parents. It is a monstrous lie, of course, but that hasn't stopped some people from believing it.

The actions must be separated from the person.

We need to begin by understanding that God created the world and all of life, including humanity, and pronounced it *good.* There is no getting around that. Because God himself is good, he could only create a good world. Since God is also love, he created this world out of love. God can be no other than goodness and love. Otherwise we are talking about something altogether different than God.

That's where we start, but we don't end there. The fact is that God gave Adam and Eve the freedom to love him back. Without that freedom, they couldn't give genuine love. It would be instinct, a response on the level of, say, that from one of their favorite lions. In this freedom Adam and Eve chose the wrong thing—essentially, to love themselves more than they did God. With that act, all of life was distorted.

Consider it like this. I am looking in a mirror when suddenly a crack appears in the middle of it. Because it is a very old mirror, the crack spiderwebs clear out to the frame on all sides. The mirror is still there. I can see myself in it. But I can see only in bits and pieces.

That's similar to what happened in what we call the Fall. Creation wasn't obliterated, but sin and evil and, yes, illness spread their way through it. In fact, Paul had much the same thing to say when he wrote in 1 Corinthians 13:12, "Now we see but a poor reflection as in a mirror; then we shall see face to face."

Life is like a cracked mirror, but we're not left there crawling among the spiderwebs. So we consider this second important point: In our fallenness, our persistent tendency to do bad things, God meets us with his persistent love and goodness. In fact, human history since Eden reveals a God never giving up on or letting go of those whom he loves.

Relate this now to the person who suffers from ADHD and who, influenced by its symptoms—impulsivity or hyperactivity, for example—has done "bad" things. I have talked with several people who were not diagnosed until their adult years. Sometimes they will look back upon and talk about their juvenile exploits with a sense of humor, but that is often a defense mechanism. One woman, not diagnosed until she was an adult, talked about the compulsive shoplifting that started when she was eight. She would simply take something on impulse, often something she had absolutely no use for, then dump it in a trash can on the way home.

More common to children with ADHD are such behaviors as playground fights, occasional eruptions in the classroom, and *many* eruptions at home. If they are able to control themselves in public situations, it seems the bad behavior gets pent up and explodes when they get on more familiar turf. They know, however, that they are acting against the rules. Consequently they genuinely feel they are being bad, or they simply accept that label to justify actions they can't understand and can hardly control.

But right here we have to understand the second important precept that challenges this myth of the "bad person." If the first three chapters of Genesis tell us how a good Creation went wrong, the entire rest of the Bible tells how the wrong is made right. It is the story of how God never forsakes his children, clutching them with the most powerful hand imaginable:

"So do not fear, for I am with you; do not be dismayed, for I am your God. I will strengthen you and help you; I will uphold you with my righteous right hand" (Is 41:10).

It is the story of how God forgives his children, restoring them to himself by pierced hands of loving mercy: "For as high as the heavens are above the earth, so great is his love for those who fear him; as far as the east is from the west, so far has he removed our transgressions from us" (Ps 103:11-12).

The story of God's grace sweeps like an avalanche of dazzling brightness through the dark spaces in his children: "For all have sinned and fall short of the glory of God, and are justified freely by his grace through the redemption that came by Christ Jesus. God presented him as a sacrifice of atonement, through faith in his blood" (Rom 3:23-25a).

And finally, it is the story of full, complete restoration of the children of God in life everlasting: "He who was seated on the throne said, 'I am making everything new!'" (Rv 21:5a).

We have two important theological precepts, then. Where do they leave us in considering the "bad person" myth? Right here:

I have an illness, but I am not the illness that I have. I am a child of God.

The No-Responsibility Myth

A second major misunderstanding is nearly the exact opposite of the first. It says that because of the illness, the person is not responsible for the actions he or she commits—"I can't help what I do because I have an illness." This is often a protective device used both by children and their parents, even by adults with ADHD, but it is also a misunderstanding that has caused enormous harm. Consider some practical examples.

It is, of course, sometimes the duty of responsible parents to inform teachers of the child's disorder. This is certainly necessary, for example, when the child's behavior is disruptive in the classroom or quarrels break out with friends. Parents do this to establish an understanding of standards of behavior for all parties, and the necessary consequences if the standards are broken.

For example, parents and a teacher might need to discuss how to approach the child for a time-out when the need arises (in a firm but soft-spoken manner, with direct eye contact, but never with physical force). Parents of the child's friends might be notified of circumstances when the parents should be called to take the child home. Granted, these actions take a lot of work, discernment, and trust, but the importance of social and moral standards has to be set at an early age.

Furthermore, to say that "my child has an illness, and there's nothing I can do about it" is a form of psychological and spiritual abandonment. Because of his or her ADHD, the child is already subject to profound questions of self-worth, a lack of personal confidence (in spite of acting out for attention), and confusion about his or her illness ("I don't know why I act that way."). If parents feel their own efforts to establish standards are failing miserably, they should certainly seek the support of a specialized counselor, and some counseling sessions should include both the parents and the child.

We are mistaken, however, if we believe that our rules, standards, and boundaries are automatic guides to well-being for the person with ADHD. Some people install electric fences—invisible since they are buried underground—to train their dogs not to wander out of the yard. This is a matter of instinct. If the dog gets popped often enough on its receiving collar, it learns not to wander.

One of the major characteristics of ADHD is difficulty with rule-governed behavior. Since impulsiveness is one characteristic of the illness, the child with ADHD might see something interesting in the neighbor's yard and impulsively run over to search it out. He or she thereby sets off, as it were, the electric shock of frustration, anger, and defiance. It is often a whirling cycle that the parents look upon in hopeless bewilderment.

The truth about the second myth, then, is this: Even if boundaries are broken, the person with ADHD must be aware that boundaries exist and that when they are overstepped, consequences result. ADHD impulsiveness will butt up against the boundaries and sometimes trample them underfoot, but the person needs to be told, "Here is where you went wrong," "These are the consequences of the actions," and, "Here is where you are safe." Then that person needs the gentle leash of forgiveness to lead him or her back to the safe place and to prop up the boundaries once more.

I have an illness. But I am not the illness that I have. I am aware of right and wrong actions, as well as the consequences of either.

The Intellectual Deficiency Myth

The third, and perhaps most damaging, misunderstanding about persons with ADHD is that they are intellectually defective.

The history of ADHD diagnosis hasn't been particularly helpful here. During the 1960s the common rubric used for ADHD was "minimal brain dysfunction." Because students with this illness often cannot perform well in the academic setting, a common opinion has it that they are just "not very bright."

There is a substantial difference between being intelligent and being able to perform adequately on that intelligence. The truly harmful nature of ADHD is that the disorder itself impedes performance. The consequences in terms of self-confidence and self-esteem are immeasurable.

The realities slash this myth to bits.

First, we have been shackled too long by the idea that our children are either "smart" or "stupid."
"Smart" or "stupid" according to what? A far better way to consider our children is to ask about their interests, gifts, and talents. For example, I'm scared of electricity. I pride myself in being a handyman, able to reroof my house, paint it flawlessly, hang wallpaper, and the like. But I look at the outlets as if they were packed full of monsters just aching to get out.

My only experience of tinkering with electricity was a bad one. I took off a light switch cover to paper a hallway and forgot to trip the circuit off in the basement. When I cut around the switch box through the wet wallpaper, I got a shock that sent me crashing into the opposite wall. When I regained my senses, I said, "Idiot!"

Yes, in that case. But I hope not in my teaching or writing or in being a loving and responsible husband and father. On the other hand, I have a younger brother who wires and repairs the electricity—hundreds of wires wrapped together—

on the massive presses at a General Motors plant. I would say he's a brilliant electrician, but I don't think I could persuade him to spend a day teaching my classes.

We have to abandon this sense of intellectual capacity as a marker of individual worth. If your child were born with one leg slightly bent and shorter than the other (as my older son was), would you be disappointed in him because he didn't win first place in his race, or would you be proud of him for finishing the race?

Second, the nature of ADHD in itself impedes academic performance according to traditional standards.
Such standards, through all levels of education, assume that in testing, a student will be able to solve a certain set of problems within a certain length of time. Whether we are talking about an individual teacher's guidelines or standardizing testing, the presumption here is one of fairness and equal limits to determine aptitude. Yet several factors inhibit an ADHD student's performance within these standards.

First, the pressure of time limits tends to confuse thought processing. While to outsiders the ADHD mind seems to be constantly scattering off onto diverse tangents, in fact it is constantly trying to *regain* focus on the task at hand. At times the person with ADHD loses that ability altogether. The thoughts, if you will, tend to wander off-track and get lost in multiple alleyways.

It is also one of the oddities of the disorder that for stretches of time a person may be capable of a nearly preternatural concentration, what is called *hyperfocus*, so that he or she becomes wholly consumed by something.

The issue here is the assumption of equitable testing standards. Often those standards are not in fact equitable for the ADHD person, who needs extra time, often twice that of assumed limits, to process responses adequately.

Second, ADHD involves a much greater than average distractibility by outside stimuli. The distracting element can be something as minor as the scratching of a pen of a student seated nearby.

Recently I had a student who took his tests in one of our testing rooms. There he not only had the extended time he needed but also the solitude he needed to talk through his tests aloud. It was a technique he had developed for keeping his focus.

Third, ADHD students may need particular routines to enable their best performance. What works best will be an individual matter, but students with ADHD have to find their own, personalized methods for imposing a degree of regularity upon academic endeavors.

For example, during my college and graduate school years (long before I was diagnosed with ADHD) I had to compose myself with meticulous routines. I started studying for exams a week before they were given. I refused to study for them on the day they were held. I tried to rest and not get distracted. I wore the same shirt and pants to every exam. I always used a fountain pen with blue ink. When I finished I never reread the exam. I never looked at grades on exams or papers until after the course was finished. I wanted to keep my focus on what I *could* achieve rather than what I might be doing wrong. I wanted to stay comfortable doing that.

At a minimum we have to understand that people with ADHD have the same intellectual *capabilities* as anyone. In terms strictly of academic testing, extended time and private quarters in a resource room should be provided. Help with outlining an essay is also beneficial.

But all this is tempered by a strong word of realism. During his or her high school years, the very worst thing that can happen to a student is to be singled out as odd or different. It is the adolescent curse. And students who already feel different because of ADHD are often going to fight furiously to protect and conceal that difference. Despite the best efforts of parents, teachers, and staff to help, they will resist—often noisily and aggressively.

Don't force them. Talk to them about options, your love, and your understanding and support. But do understand that these young people are already uncertain about themselves, and more than anything need support in the belief that while they might have a disorder, they are not mental defectives of any sort.

TWO

What It Is

Pete (all names are fictional) is one of several college-age students I interviewed at length for this project. It seemed to me that college-age students are a nearly ideal group for consideration. They have achieved an adult-level understanding of their illness but are still close enough to their childhood and adolescence to remember what it was like growing up with the illness of ADHD.

As he sits across from me at the circular table in my office, Pete appears wholly at ease, one leg crossed over the knee of the other, unconsciously jiggling one foot. His fingers drum lightly on the table surface.

Pete starts with middle school, where his dislike of school began to intensify dramatically. He felt, he said, "like I couldn't comprehend anything."

"What do you mean by that?"

"When I read the assignments, I couldn't follow them. I didn't know what to do. And I couldn't follow what the teacher said in class. My mind would always be drifting off."

"About what?"

"I don't even know. It was like … I wasn't even there. And then, because I wasn't following the stuff, I'd get anxious before tests. Really anxious. I didn't want to be in school at all."

Pete's academic world, despite his best efforts, seemed to get more out of control in high school. He felt a constant need to be doing things, but he kept forgetting to do the things he was supposed to do. He couldn't keep the pieces of his life straight, and priorities were lost on him. He began leaving Post-It notes all over, but he'd still forget appointments. It seemed he couldn't organize anything at all.

His parents tried to help him. They encouraged him and gave him a lot of "positive feedback," helping him with reminders to get work done.

During his first semester of college, things got entirely out of control. For the first time Pete was faced with the real possibility of flunking out, and that reality pushed him into a depression such that he could hardly function at all.

Fortunately Pete sought help, with the support of his parents. First he consulted the counseling center at the college, then a psychologist who could test for ADHD. After that he was referred to a physician.

He was first given a prescription for Ritalin, but that was changed to Adderall, a longer-lasting stimulant, in combination with the antidepressant Effexor. Pete felt tremendous relief, first from being able to identify his illness and then from having found an effective treatment for it, one that made him feel better.

While Pete had come a long way, he still had a way to go. In order to cope with his illness, he had to learn to rearrange his entire life. The first of the solutions he put into practice might surprise some people.

"Be very guarded," Pete said, "whom you talk with. You see,

if people hear that you have ADHD, they right away assume you're taking Ritalin."

"Yes," I said, "but more often now doctors prescribe Adderall so you don't have to be on the rigorous schedule."

"Exactly. But they still *assume* you're taking Ritalin. And they'll be after you to buy it."

"Stay awake to study?"

"Right. There's a whole black market for Ritalin. One of my friends had a whole new prescription stolen out of his room. And what a hassle he had to replace it."

"What other strategies do you use, Pete?"

"I continue with my support group at the counseling center. I use a planner. Everything goes into the planner. The coach of my support group helps me plan out each week so I have all my appointments, tests, and stuff like that scheduled. And I have to schedule study time.

"Probably the most important thing to me is that I've just plain had to simplify my lifestyle. I realize I can't do everything I want to do. So I've learned to set priorities."

In many ways, and despite the turmoil of his youth, Pete's is a happy story. He was accurately diagnosed, effective medications were prescribed, and a new lifestyle was adopted.

Most important, however, is the fact that he learned to accept his illness and manage his life to live with it. He is outgoing, personable, and happy. With effort, his grades have improved to the point where he feels for the first time in his life that he is living up to his "potential."

Understanding ADHD

Understanding of the illness itself, however, is the crucial first step in reaching a satisfactory adjustment to living with ADHD. Without getting bogged down in too much medical terminology, it is important that we walk that first step too.

Frequency

Most studies indicate that ADHD affects approximately 5 percent of all children in the United States. That's slightly over two million.

According to a 1994 report from the National Institute of Mental Health (NIMH), ADHD affects about two to three times more boys than girls. These figures vary, however, as specialists determine the degree of severity of the illness, from mild to severe. The former can often be handled with behavioral management, while the latter calls for immediate medical intervention.

History of Our Understanding

The question is often raised whether ADHD is overdiagnosed in the U.S. and whether the primary medicine, Ritalin, is overprescribed. The answers are somewhat ambiguous, but it is clear that the U.S. developed diagnostic criteria well before other countries. These criteria have permitted medical professionals to intervene quickly and accurately.

Our understanding of the disorder that we now call ADHD has evolved through several crucial phases over fifty years of medical research. In the 1940s, for example, there was an outbreak of encephalitis that did in fact leave its younger victims brain-damaged. For about twenty years following that, children having traits of ADHD were labeled "minimally brain-damaged." The term was, in and of itself, damaging enough.

During the early 1960s, however, psychiatrists took note of the fact that the difficult behavior occurred in situations when there was absolutely no evidence of brain trauma or illness. Therefore they coined the term "minimal brain dysfunction." The term was something of a cover-up. *How* was the brain not functioning fully? And *why*?

Studies continued to sharpen understanding. In 1980, the standard reference text, *Diagnostic and Statistical Manual of Mental Disorders, Third Edition (DSM-111),*[1] made clarifying distinctions between ADHD and Attention Deficit Disorder (ADD). These distinguished between those who are primarily hyperactive and those who are primarily inattentive. The *DSM-III* also clearly listed traits that identified the two illnesses.

The *DSM-IV,*[2] published in 1994 and revised in 2000, combined ADHD and ADD into ADHD, now the preferred name. But it also distinguished between three categories of ADHD:

1. ADHD primarily inattentive (less hyperactive)
2. ADHD primarily hyperactive and impulsive
3. ADHD combined type

Chapter three, "Tools for Diagnosis," will examine the means by which a doctor arrives at these diagnoses.

The Roots of ADHD

One final part of this puzzle that is ADHD remains: Where does it come from? The question is indeed puzzling, for medical science to this date isn't entirely certain. Nonetheless, medical studies do supply three key possibilities.

Genetic Influences

In 1990, President George Bush and the U.S. Congress, as directed by leading mental health agencies in Washington, declared the decade of the 1990s the "Decade of the Brain." Fueled by funds for research and guided by concentrated and coordinated studies, medical science uncovered more about the intricate marvels of brain function than perhaps was found in all of prior history.

One of the key discoveries about mental disorders was the role of genetic transmission (or family history of an illness). It was learned that disorders such as ADHD frequently have a genetic history. The same is true, for example, with depressive disorders.

Several cautions are necessary. First, this discovery is only an aid in diagnosis. Its value is that it promotes quicker diagnosis and appropriate medical intervention.

If one or both parents have a diagnosed disorder, and if a child exhibits characteristics of the disorder as listed in the *DSM-IV*, the *likelihood* of the child having inherited a genetically based biochemical makeup that would support that disorder is greater. It does *not* mean, however, that the children of such parents will inevitably inherit the disorder. The likelihood is *greater*, but the inheriting is *not* inevitable.

These discoveries also bring light to another problem, that is, diagnosis of ADHD in adults. The fact of the matter is that previous generations were not adequately screened and diagnosed for the illness. What happened to those untreated persons? Too often they dropped out of high school, frustrated and confused by their inability to concentrate, and entered the work force. In adult life many were afflicted with bouts of depression or a general low level of dysthymia (mild but persistent day-to-day depression). Some turned to alcohol, marijuana, or other drugs to calm the mind. And some managed, somehow, intuitively to adopt coping mechanisms that permitted them to survive. In some instances the latter groups even managed to harness the wild energies common to ADHD to achieve success in their fields.

The improved diagnostic tools now being employed with children are in turn being employed to help their parents. The importance of realizing the genetic connection is underscored by a report from Dr. Joseph Beiderman, one of the country's foremost experts on ADHD. In an address to the 1996 Conference of Children and Adults with Attention-Deficit/Hyperactivity Disorder (CHADD), he stated that children with ADHD have a 500 percent greater probability of having an immediate relative with the illness than a child without ADHD.

Biochemical Brain Activity

The second important area of discovery during the past decade has been that of brain chemistry. Where learning about the genetic relationships has been of great help in diagnosis, this new knowledge has given us a much greater appreciation of what is actually going on in the brain that produces ADHD. This understanding, in turn, leads to better medical treatment of the disorder.

Basically, study of the brain's biochemical functions tells us what it is that is genetically inherited. These two areas of knowledge, taken together, do much to help us gain the kind of understanding that will enable us to cope with living with ADHD day to day.

As we address this subject, it is not necessary to go into fine scientific detail. The processes can be understood in a simplified manner. We also need to remember that the subject is still under intense medical study, which constantly turns up new information and directions. Even if we celebrate the 1990s as the "Decade of the Brain," the study started then has not stopped.

The basics of recent findings are as follows. Studies of the metabolism of the brain in ADHD patients indicate decreased activity in three essential neurotransmitters: serotonin, norepinephrine, and dopamine. These chemicals transmit messages from one nerve cell to another. When they fail to function normally, both mood and brain activity are affected.

Consider first the effect on mood. These same neurotransmitters, researchers have discovered, affect depression and bipolar depression disorders. Many of the so-called "designer" antidepressant drugs of the last decade have been targeted at producing a smooth flow and reuptake of the chemicals between nerve cells. In fact, several of these drugs, including Tofranil, Norpramin, and Effexor, for example, have been found to be particularly helpful for ADHD and are often prescribed in addition to a stimulant.

Medical treatment of ADHD. Stimulants are the main pharmaceutical course of treatment for ADHD. The intention is to stimulate the neurotransmitters dopamine and norepinephrine into normal function. This stimulation helps control hyperactivity, impulsivity, and inability to concentrate.

The most common drugs used to create this stimulation include the following:

Ritalin. This brand-name version of methyl phenidate may be the best known of the drugs useful in ADHD treatment and for a long time was the only one offered. The standard dosage of Ritalin affects behavior for three to four hours. It works quickly and has a good safety record. Some of the side effects include weight loss, insomnia, headaches, and decreased appetite. See also Appendix A, "The Ritalin Controversy."

Ritalin-SR. This is an extended-duration form of Ritalin. It is effective for approximately seven hours. It is particularly useful for students who are embarrassed by taking medicines during the school day, or for use at schools without proper procedures for drug administration.

Concerta. This is a relatively new stimulant, released in August 2000. Concerta is designed as a "once a day" extended release of methyl phenidate. One tablet swallowed in the morning begins to release immediately and continues for twelve hours. It appears to be meeting with excellent success, both in duration and by having minimal side effects.

Dexedrine (dextroamphetamine). This stimulant is another that can be prescribed either in a short-acting (three to four hours) or longer-lasting (seven to eight hours) form. Like Ritalin, it has a good safety record and shares many of the same side effects.

Adderall. This is a combination drug (dextroamphetamine and amphetamine) that also works as a stimulant to the central nervous system. Its primary value is that it comes in a longer-acting form than Ritalin or Dexedrine, although, as an amphetamine, it shares similar side effects.

Cylert (pemoline). This drug has the advantage of a twelve- to twenty-four-hour duration, but it takes two to four weeks to achieve a clinical response. In contrast, Ritalin, Dexedrine, and Adderall are effective quickly. Cylert use requires regular blood tests to monitor possible effects on liver function.

Doctors recognize that a holistic approach to treating ADHD is needed. In addition to the stimulant drugs, counseling is appropriate. Doctors also often prescribe an antidepressant to help the person deal with the emotional devastation of the illness. Three antidepressants in particular have shown good results with ADHD:

Tofranil (imipramine). This is one of the antidepressants in the class known as tricyclics. It targets some of the same brain chemistry that is involved in ADHD. It has the typical side effects of antidepressants, including dry mouth, blurred vision, and dizziness. Generally, the side effects disappear in a few weeks.

Norpramin (desipramine). This is also a tricyclic antidepressant. It particularly addresses a deficiency in the neurotransmitters norepinephrine and serotonin.

Effexor (venlafaxine). This is a unique drug, both in chemistry and effect. It targets all three neurotransmitters, is quickly and easily absorbed by the body, and in most people has minimal side effects, the most common being anxiety or sleeplessness.[3]

Why some don't take medication. Frankly, talk of drugs that affect the operations of the brain scares the living daylights out of many people. Many young people refuse to take medications. "I want to be the real me," they say. I can't count the number of times I have heard that. I point out that medications *enable* you to be the person you really are, the person God designed you to be. Yet many of them prefer to suffer the chaotic pain of ADHD and the suffering of depression in order to be the "real me."

Perhaps this objection can best be answered by an analogy. I am one of those fortunate people (living in Michigan as I do) who rarely gets the flu. Several years can go by before some bug finds me attractive. I feel slightly superior to the lesser mortals until that bug bites. Then it exacts revenge for my assumed superiority. It cuts off my legs at the knees, leaves me gasping for breath and burning with fever. I don't feel for a second like my "real self." But I'm not altogether stupid. Michigan teaches one how to deal with the flu: copious amounts of water, hot tea, vitamin C, and buckets of Tylenol. And sleep. In about four days I feel like my "real self" again.

I've never understood why we're quick to get medical help for physical problems but dangerously slow for psychological ones. People don't want to admit that "there's something wrong with my brain." I wonder if these same people would try to walk around on a broken leg. Would that be the "real me"?

There are also people who have spiritual objections to taking psychotropic drugs. They feel that doing so would be to fail to rely on God—to be placing their trust in false things, if you will.

Does the illness of ADHD (and its frequent companions, depression and anxiety) make you feel closer to God or further away? I can recall periods when my ADHD was particularly bad (during periods of stress) and, when I would try to have my morning devotions, I would have absolutely no sense of what I was doing. It was as if I were lost in a large hollow space. If anything, the use of proper medications has brought me closer to God.

Environmental Causes

The role of certain environmental factors in producing ADHD has received increased attention in recent years. We know that nicotine, illicit drugs, and alcohol can all affect fetal development. Alcohol and nicotine, according to NIMH studies, may distort developing nerve cells in the brain. Fetal Alcohol Syndrome (FAS) may cause children to show many of the signs of ADHD. Use of drugs such as cocaine, or its smokable equivalent, crack, affects the brain cells that are receptors to neurotransmitters.

Identifying these three kinds of possible cause does not necessarily mean that any given individual whose parent used, or who himself or herself uses, such a substance will have ADHD. Knowing about them, however, increases the possibility of quick and effective intervention by an experienced professional.

A Final Note

We have to protect ourselves from the error of diagnosing ourselves or others based on peripheral evidence. That is to say, if one sibling has ADHD, parents might assume all other siblings do. This requires a professional diagnosis. If a child is rather "high-strung" or active, one might assume the child has ADHD. In fact, that may just be the child's native temperament. Further guides are needed. In the next chapter, we'll explore some of the additional guidelines professionals use for diagnosis.

THREE

Tools for Diagnosis

Elise, a college senior, is one of those naturally attractive and personable people with whom one immediately feels comfortable. She is so quick to smile and so calm and articulate in her responses that it is difficult to imagine the tangled and painful path of her young life.

One would think Elise had an advantage. Her father, after all, is a highly regarded psychiatrist, and it is true that he detected signs of his daughter's distress early in high school. He referred her to a colleague, who prescribed the antidepressant Prozac. It seemed a reasonable choice. But then suddenly and without apparent reason, Elise's moods would swing down like a plane falling from the sky.

Elise formed her own opinions. She fought taking medication. In her own words, she "wanted to be normal." Indeed, that seems to be the heartfelt plea of every adolescent. At best, Elise took her medicines when she remembered, or when she cared to, which created a dizzying roller coaster of chemical processes in her brain. Finally she gave it all up to do whatever felt right to her.

I am amazed by how calmly she talks to me about it. I wonder if it hurts her. But her deep brown eyes never leave mine. Her voice is strong. It is not the first time I have heard such things. I believe her. Perhaps that is why she doesn't hesitate.

"My academics finally just fell apart," she said. "I think teachers just passed me along for my parents' sake. I couldn't seem to ever finish a project. I'd write maybe a page in study hall, then forget to finish it when I got home."

"Did you turn it in?" I asked.

"Oh, sure. But I always had this panic the next morning. Like, 'Oh, the report is due. And I only have one page written.'"

Elise didn't so much give up as she rebelled. There were more exciting things to do than one page of a ten-page theme. Her entire lifestyle changed dramatically. With the "help" of some new friends, she discovered a grunge shop. Her expensive wardrobe lay tossed aside in a closet. She adopted the whole lifestyle—piercings, a tattoo—seemingly overnight.

"I imagine your parents were a bit dismayed," I said.

For the first time she averted her glance and paused. "I don't know how I would have made it without them," she said. "Even at my worst, they loved me and stood by me."

"What do you mean by 'my worst'?"

"The whole scene that follows that lifestyle. When you start to rebel, you get caught up in it. Alcohol, drugs, sex." She stated it flatly, without evasion. It was part of the reality.

"What happened?"

"Somehow I did really want to go to college," Elise said. "I was excited about it. In my freshman year, though, I just couldn't manage the work. I was miserable. I wanted to drop out."

Elise realized that she needed help, and she knew that medication would be necessary to be "normal." She submitted to psychological testing, which did reveal ADHD. She has now been taking Adderall since her freshman year and knows she might be taking it indefinitely. She also takes an antidepressant during peak stress periods. For example, she starts the additional medication several weeks before exams, as a precautionary measure.

What practical solutions or suggestions does Elise have to offer us? Like Pete, she keeps a careful weekly planner, but she finds it necessary to expand it to include a daily *To Do* list. Elise crosses out each item as she finishes it.

Her list includes the specific times for scheduled medications. "It's so easy to miss," she said. "Or to get an hour or two late. Then I wonder what to do." She also schedules both the time and place where she will study. Elise found that if she didn't schedule a place that felt comfortable, she would just wander around until the study time was done.

One other thing was necessary. Elise schedules free time just to have coffee with friends, to "hit the mall," or to go out for an evening. She finds that because she has it scheduled, she doesn't worry about all the other things she might have to be doing.

Also like Pete, Elise doesn't feel it's necessary to make her illness generally known to others. She feels she has learned to live with it. In fact, while reflecting upon her life with ADHD, Elise commented that her years since diagnosis had involved an important personal learning experience. "With the medications," she said, "I see that I now *can* learn. I'm not dumb. I have a sense of conquering my illness just by learning to live with it."

In the previous chapter we looked at some possible causes for ADHD. But how does the medical community know if someone actually has it? How can a doctor talk with Elise in her junior year of high school, see past the pierced eyebrows, the spiral multicolored hair, the black, spiked collar at her neck, and separate her from someone engaged in teenage rebellion (a bit to the extreme) from someone who has an illness?

In the same way that a reddened nose, a hacking cough, and a fever of 102° might suggest to a doctor that you have a viral infection, so too certain indicators signal the presence of ADHD.

There are two primary methods of testing for ADHD. A psychologist (Ph.D.) specializing in the area is likely to administer diagnostic checklist tests, followed by discussion. A psychiatrist (M.D.) might use some of the same tools, or he can formulate a generalized diagnosis through evaluation sessions, family history, and personal medical history. His or her major resource will be the *DSM-IV* list of indicators.

Psychologists and psychiatrists are not in separate camps, of course. As a general rule they work closely together. If a psychologist determines that a person has ADHD, the person is referred to a medical doctor for evaluation and the prescription and oversight of medication. In turn, the doctor may refer the person back to the psychologist for work on coping strategies for living with ADHD.

In describing diagnostic strategies, however, several cautions must be held up. In their national bestseller, *Driven to Distraction,*[1] medical doctors Edward Hallowell and John Ratey point out two major concerns. Even with reliance upon testing tools, they say, these particular errors in diagnosis often take place: missing the diagnosis or making a diagnosis too often.

Missing ADHD occurs because even professionals—teachers, psychologists, and medical doctors—simply do not know enough about the disorder. Even with testing the diagnosis can be missed. This occurs, the authors argue, because, "while much psychological testing can be very helpful, it is not *definitive.*"[2]

One problem is that the process of testing itself can create a focus a person doesn't have on a day-to-day basis. This is especially true for children. During normal schoolwork, a child might focus on creative tasks or on repetitive, long-range drills. A psychological test generally calls for more rapid response and unaccustomed focus.

On the other hand, ADHD might be diagnosed for a set of conditions that only mimic the illness, leading to overdiagnosis. For example, the medical condition of hyperthyroidism can produce ADHD-like symptoms. A thorough medical exam and blood tests should be included in any diagnostic procedure.

Fortunately, the *DSM-IV* furnishes guidelines to protect against overdiagnosis in children:

1. Are the ADHD-like behaviors persistent?
2. Are they maladaptive (faulty or inadequate adaptation to tasks or surroundings) or inappropriate for the developmental level?
3. Are they evident in at least two settings?
4. Do they impair social, academic, or, for adults, psychological testing?

5. Do they occur at times other than during psychological testing?
6. Have other mental and physical disorders been ruled out?

With such guidelines in mind, psychologists might use a variety of testing techniques in addition to talking with the patient. In the case of children, parents might be asked to place their child's behaviors on a continuum, as by describing each behavior with "not at all," "a little," "pretty much," or "very much." The behaviors they are asked to evaluate in this way might include:

> Is restless, always moving around.
> Fails to finish things.
> Talks back to grown-ups.
> Becomes frustrated with tasks.
> Has temper outbursts.
> Fights with friends.
> Has problems sleeping.

A typical questionnaire might have anywhere from fifty to one hundred such statements and helps analyze behavior patterns. The behavior patterns are then compared to those known to typify ADHD.

The standard *DSM-IV* approach is to measure the *presence* and *persistence* of certain symptoms. For example, in diagnosing ADHD in children, the *DSM-IV* recommends the observation for six months of eight or more symptoms out of its diagnostic criteria for ADHD.

Diagnostic Criteria
Attention-Deficit/Hyperactivity Disorder

A. Either (1) or (2):

(1) six (or more) of the following symptoms of **inattention** have persisted for at least six months to a degree that is maladaptive and inconsistent with developmental level:

Inattention

(a) often fails to give close attention to details or makes careless mistakes in schoolwork, work, or other activities

(b) often has difficulty sustaining attention in tasks or play activities

(c) often does not seem to listen when spoken to directly

(d) often does not follow through on instructions and fails to finish schoolwork, chores, or duties in the workplace (not due to oppositional behavior or failure to understand instructions)

(e) often has difficulty organizing tasks and activities

(f) often avoids, dislikes, or is reluctant to engage in tasks that require sustained mental effort (such as schoolwork or homework)

(g) often loses things necessary for tasks or activities (e.g., toys, school assignments, pencils, books, or tools)

(h) often is easily distracted by extraneous stimuli

(i) often is forgetful in daily activities

(2) six (or more) of the following symptoms of **hyperactivity-impulsivity** have persisted for at least six months to a degree that is maladaptive and inconsistent with developmental level:

Hyperactivity
(a) often fidgets with hands or feet or squirms in seat
(b) often leaves seat in classroom or in other situations in which remaining seated is expected
(c) often runs about or climbs excessively in situations in which it is inappropriate (in adolescents or adults, may be limited to subjective feelings of restlessness)
(d) often has difficulty playing or engaging in leisure activities quietly
(e) often is "on the go" or often acts as if "driven by a motor"
(f) often talks excessively

Impulsivity
(g) often blurts out answers before questions have been completed
(h) often has difficulty awaiting turn
(i) often interrupts or intrudes on others (e.g., butts into conversations or games)

B. Some hyperactive-impulsive or inattentive symptoms that caused impairment were before age seven years.

C. Some impairment from the symptoms is present in two or more settings (e.g., at school [or work] and at home).

D. There must be clear evidence of clinically significant impairment in social, academic, or occupational functioning.

E. The symptoms do not occur exclusively during the course of a Pervasive Developmental Disorder, Schizophrenia, or other Psychotic Disorder and are not better accounted for by another mental disorder (e.g., Mood Disorder, Anxiety Disorder, Dissociative Disorder, or a Personality Disorder).

Code based on type:

314.01 **Attention-Deficit/Hyperactivity Disorder, Combined Type:** If both Criteria A1 and A2 are met for the past six months

314.00 **Attention-Deficit/Hyperactivity Disorder, Predominantly Inattentive Type:** If Criterion A1 is met but Criterion A2 is not met for the past six months

314.01 **Attention-Deficit/Hyperactivity Disorder, Predominantly Hyperactive-Impulsive Type:** If Criterion A2 is met but Criterion A1 is not met for the past six months[3]

While such measures of symptom criteria are fundamental to diagnosis, they are far from the only resource. Perhaps at the head of the list would be the parents' observations about life in the home. Sometimes, by enormous effort, the ADHD child can keep his or her emotions bottled up in the classroom. Once home from school, the bottle bursts apart. The child "acts out" all the pent-up effects of the day. ADHD can be one of the disorders most disruptive of home life. Often that's because the child believes this is a safe place to let it all hang out.

It's also a place where parents can get all strung out.

Having examined what the illness is, and how it is diagnosed, we turn now to the harder issue: how to live with it.

FOUR

Living With ADHD

In the previous chapter, on diagnosing ADHD, I made an analogy between having a viral infection and having ADHD. That is to say, certain indicators or symptoms lead to a diagnosis of the flu. So too certain indicators or symptoms lead to a diagnosis of ADHD. Beyond that, however, the analogy breaks down completely.

We all know what to do with the flu: get plenty of rest, drink plenty of fluids, and take an analgesic for the fever, aches, and pains. Then, after a week or so, you're over it.

Unfortunately, for ADHD there is no being "over it." The disorder is *managed*, not cured. The solution lies in recognizing one has the disorder and then learning to live with it. In this regard, ADHD is more like diabetes mellitus, a chronic metabolic disorder that requires close attention to what and when one eats, close monitoring of blood sugar levels, and regular injections of insulin throughout one's life.

Consider here two young adults who had to learn this illness management.

Susan

Among the students I interviewed, the average age of diagnosis for ADHD was in the sixteen to eighteen range. It was then that parents began to throw up their hands and wonder if something more than "troubled" behavior was going on with their child. Susan, however, was diagnosed in third grade. She remembers it clearly but not happily.

Oh, she was terrified of school, this young Susan. "I hated school as far back as I can remember," she said. "I'd get sick before school. I'd cry every morning."

"Why?"

"Because I couldn't *do* anything the other kids did."

"Can you remember an example?"

She thought for a moment, then grinned.

"This is all the way back to kindergarten. We each had to make a train of colored paper. I think we were learning colors and numbers. Anyway, all the other kids quickly finished and went out to recess. I couldn't go out to recess until I finished that dumb train."

Susan thought for a minute. "I could never finish things," she said.

By the third grade her trauma over school became so intense that her parents took her to a child psychologist. Although Susan was diagnosed with ADHD, the psychologist and her family doctor were reluctant to start her on stimulant medicines. This may have been, in part, due to the fact that far less was known at that time about how stimulants functioned in brain chemistry. Many professionals were cautious in treating such young children. Instead Susan was engaged in behavioral therapy and what she called "special learning."

The latter is the subject of some debate. In Susan's case it meant that, starting in third grade, she went to a walled-off area of the classroom to finish her work in "individual time." Later it meant such accommodations as the use of a resource room for study and testing. Susan welcomed the resources. It was much more important to her to be able to finish her task successfully than to worry about social stigma. She seems to be one of those rare individuals who freely accepted and readily adapted to her illness.

"I just didn't have any hang-ups about it," she says with a grin. "In fact, in high school I wrote an essay and gave a talk on how I overcame the illness."

"How was that?"

"By living an organized lifestyle! I even had to be taught how to clear my desk for study. And *no* music. Not even noise. If I hear something, it's like a switch flips in my brain and all my attention goes there."

"You seem to be pretty open about having ADHD. How do you deal with other people who may have questions?"

"I answer them. I admit I have an illness. I *have* to admit that. I have to live with it. And I can."

"You certainly do seem to have adapted well. Have you ever had medicine prescribed?"

"I started Ritalin for about a month in grade school. I remember that I couldn't sleep, and it made me nervous."

"So then you relied on coaching and adapting techniques. Any medicines since then?"

For the first time I saw a shadow of a frown pass over Susan's face. At first I thought she wasn't going to answer, and I was ready to let the question drop.

"In high school," she said suddenly, "I became quite depressed when I was about fifteen, and I took Wellbutrin [an antide-pressant] for a little over a year."

"That doesn't surprise me," I said.

"No?"

"No. For one thing you were at a critical phase of adoles-cence. The body is changing physically and hormonally. There are new psychological challenges every day—friends, future, family. The famous three *F*s."

She laughed then.

"Also," I said, "ADHD ties into some of the same brain chemistry, particularly dopamine, as does depression. So you see, it wasn't really so surprising. But it sure looks to me as if you've managed wonderfully."

Susan is one of those wonderful, but relatively rare, case studies. From early childhood she seems to have developed a very strong self-understanding. She understood that she had a disorder, but with a rare maturity she determined early on to find measures to manage it. She has done so successfully. As Susan was leaving my office, she made a remark that struck me. I had heard it repeated one way or another by every per-son I had talked with so far. "I couldn't have made it without my parents' support," she said as she stepped out the doorway.

This comment is worth pausing over. ADHD can wreak havoc in the household, trying the patience of all involved in the family. Moreover, siblings often wonder why Child X receives special "privileges." We make no mistake about the psychological toll that the demands of an ADHD child can make. Not only does the impulsivity and hyperactivity often appear more pronounced in the "safer" confines of the home, but also the daily living environment of the child may appear on the edge of chaos. Clothes may be strewn about the bedroom. Toys clutter the floor. And, of course, turning lights off seldom enters their minds. When they leave a room, they just leave. In broad daylight every light can be lit. Sometimes the effort to structure boundaries coupled with giving the child loving guidance can seem purely overwhelming.

What Susan and the others were confessing to, though, is a certain knowledge that they wouldn't be abandoned. No matter how low they thought of themselves, no matter how fiercely they tested the limits or grew defiant, they had a sense of steady, unfailing love.

Those of us who experience ADHD in our households know well the family trauma that the illness can create. Our patience is stretched to, and sometimes beyond, the breaking point. Sometimes we just want to get in the car and drive away for a few hours, but we're afraid what condition the house will be in when we return. Will clothing be strewn all over? Any holes kicked in the walls?

As persons who have ADHD or as parents who are raising an ADHD child, we have to remember two very important things. First, despite our best use of boundaries, the ADHD child will, like a storm bent on destruction, slam against them—some children harder than others. The confusion and tensions of a child dealing with this disorder sometimes simply explode.

Second, we parents have to remind ourselves once again that our child is not bad (although he or she may be doing bad things and has to be held accountable for that). Then we have to remember that we are not therefore "bad" parents.

How often haven't we had that thought, *How have I gone wrong, to fail so miserably?* Believe me, the frequent home life chaos produced by ADHD is little reflection of one's parenting skills. It requires patience as broad as an ocean and as tough as the granite shoreline cliffs.

Several years ago, Dr. Harold Koplewicz, a well-known child and adolescent psychiatrist, published a book aptly titled *It's Nobody's Fault.*[1] He raises all the old problems of the blame game. If your child has asthma, are you, the parents, blamed for bad parenting skills? If your child gets in trouble in second grade—fidgeting, blurting out answers—you're possibly blamed for being a bad parent. No discipline, you know. They let that kid Jimmy do whatever he wants. Meanwhile, Jimmy comes home from a disastrous day in second grade. He blames himself! So he acts out further at home. Jimmy's frustrated parents can't understand why their child never behaves. Of course they're to blame. They're doing something wrong. Or at least not doing something right. But they don't know what it is.

Do you see what happened? We're right back at the beginning of this vicious cycle called the blame game.

Dr. Koplewicz sticks a heavy wrench into all the cogs of the cycle, stops the machinery, and declares, "It's Nobody's Fault." To be sure, there *are* responsibilities. If your child's brain chemistry ("wiring," some people call it) produces behavior that fits ADHD symptomology, dutiful and loving parents seek help for that child. That is part of their responsibility. But they are not responsible for the disorder itself. In this fallen world, where things go awry despite our best efforts, ADHD enters the human experience in the same way as diabetes, Lou Gehrig's disease, multiple sclerosis, and polio do. Dr. Koplewicz writes that ADHD and related disorders "exist not because of what a child's parents do but because of how his brain works, the brain that he was born with.... A child's brain disorder is not his parents' fault. It's nobody's fault."[2]

Bradley

If Susan was diagnosed and treated for ADHD at a relatively young age, learning to manage her life with helpful guidelines, Bradley's life has a few more twists and turns.

Brad is a slight, interesting young man, a junior in college. He is handsome, dark-complected, and articulate. He wears gold-rimmed granny glasses over his dark eyes, giving him a scholarly appearance. Indeed, he maintains a 3.5 grade point average and is an honors student in the business curriculum.

His aim in life is entirely clear to him. Upon graduation he wants to enter the mission field, working to set up indigenous businesses. In fact, he grew up in Nigeria. It was there that he underwent therapy for stuttering (completely nonevident now), and his speech therapist first detected signs of what she determined to be ADD.

Despite his obvious intelligence his ninth grade course work had not gone well, and in tenth grade his family physician placed Brad on Ritalin for six months. No formal testing was done, but he seemed to respond well. He never was a discipline problem. In fact, when one of his friends saw the bottle of Ritalin in Brad's locker once, he couldn't believe that he needed the medication. After the short-term use of Ritalin, Brad seemed to function fine for the rest of high school.

In college the floor dropped out from under him. There was a dark, bewildering space under him, and Brad was left in a directionless maze. Because of his obvious aptitude and scholarships, he had been enrolled in honors courses at the college. The sheer volume of reading overwhelmed him. It seemed that the harder he tried to focus, the more he lost concentration. After initial testing he was referred to a medical doctor specializing in diagnosis and treatment of ADHD. With the use of Adderall, Brad's life began to turn around.

In some ways Brad was fortunate. His diagnosis focused upon his inattentiveness and his inability to concentrate under stress. He never had the behavioral problems associated with hyperactivity and impulsivity. But he had a firm, clear sense of what solutions he required to manage his life. Without hesitation he listed them.

"First," he said, "my parents were heavily involved right from the start. Way back when I was getting therapy in Nigeria, they worked with the therapist and me. They were my primary support, really.

"Second, I had strong structure and discipline in my life growing up. My parents both taught at the boarding school that I attended. A boarding school is," he paused and laughed, "sort of a cross between one big family and a military camp. But you're close there, with the students and the teachers. They're all your family.

"Now," he added, "I've found my greatest need is still for organization."

As with each of the students I interviewed, Brad had found that living with ADHD is learning to manage it. Planned organization is the starting point.

In Susan and Brad we find two examples of people who have learned to live with ADHD through a combination of medicine and careful management of time and activities. Although their individual stories are unique to their experience, they are representative of many of the students I interviewed.

James

I had not planned to include the story of James here, yet I believe there's an obligation to do so. You see, James is still struggling in stages of denial of his illness. There can't be management until there is acceptance.

James is a burly, strong young man of twenty-one. He smiles easily, but there seems to be an indefinable edge of tension flickering behind his blue eyes. During our interview, his glance would be penetrating for a moment, then dart off.

It was a sturdy chair there, across from me at the round table. I thought James was going to capsize it. From the second he sat in it, he couldn't sit still—foot jittering over one knee, a sudden shift in posture every minute or so, fingers pulling a crossed foot or drumming on the table. If James had been a package of fireworks, I would have cleared out.

I try to keep my office professional but also as comfortable as possible for students. Next to the round table stands a 1930s Philco upright radio that I restored. Windows are lined with plants. Odd mementos—Petosky stones, eucalyptus pods, gifts from former students, like my ceramic coffee mug—all have their place. Photos of family are hung near my desk. A comfortable place. It seemed like a jail cell to James.

After some small talk, I asked him my standard opening question: "When were you first diagnosed, James?"

"Not until I was eighteen. Between high school and college."

"And you're how old now?"

"Twenty-one. But I'm not sure I'm what you're looking for."

"What do you mean, James? I'm really just doing what researchers do. You know, investigate the evidence and see if it leads to conclusions."

A shift in his seat. A glance out the window. Legs recrossed. "No." He chuckled, still looking out the window. "No, I'm sure you know what you're doing, but the e-mail [through the counseling center] mentioned ADHD. I only have ADD. I need some help studying and taking tests."

"I see." Now it was my turn to turn away. James took advantage of the opportunity to stand up and stretch.

"James, why don't we just consider some questions, okay? The different terms might not be so important right now."

As we talked it became clear that James nearly perfectly fit the *DSM-IV* profile for ADHD—impulsivity and hyperactivity. But what went wrong? Here he was, twenty-one years old and in full denial of an illness that he had to learn to manage.

Following his cue, I asked him when he first became aware of his difficulty taking tests and studying.

"I really noticed it myself," James said, "when I started studying Spanish in eighth grade. I thought it was going to be the easiest language. All the smart kids took Latin or French, you know?"

I didn't know about that, but it said a lot about James' *perception of himself.*

"Okay," I said. "How did it go for you?"

"Horrible. I couldn't make sense of the simplest things. I was at my best friend's house one afternoon trying to study with him. His mother was home, and maybe she was listening in. She's a psychiatrist. Anyway, she talked with me then about my schoolwork."

I waited a minute while James shifted several times in his chair. It seemed he wanted to quit. I offered him a Coke, asked if he wanted to take a break.

"No. That's okay. My friend's mom called my mom—she's divorced—and suggested that maybe some testing would be helpful."

"What happened then?"

"For my mom, testing meant medicine. She hates the idea of medicines. She thinks, and still thinks, that people are misdiagnosed all the time and given too much medicine. 'Drugged up,' she called it."

"I see. Then what happened?"

"I really started getting in trouble. I was always a pretty big kid, see. But between eighth and ninth grades it seemed I was always getting in fights. I'd have run-ins with the police—minor stuff, you know. I couldn't control my temper. Same thing in the classroom in ninth grade. If I could mess something up, I would. The funny thing was, the more I did that the more depressed I got about myself."

"Sort of like you didn't want to behave that way but couldn't help it?"

"Exactly. I hated the way I was."

For the first time since he walked in, James sat quietly. It was almost as if he feared reaching this point, and now having reached it could finally relax a bit.

"I can understand that, James."

"You can?"

"It's not unusual. You do things that you don't want to do, and you can't understand why you do them. It's like a trigger goes off in your brain and you can't switch it back. Since you know the things you do are wrong—or bad—you start feeling like you're just a bad person."

"I was a bad person."

"A dirty rotten scoundrel?"

"Are you making fun of me?"

"Not at all, James. But I think it's important for you to understand that while you may have done bad things, you're not a bad person. A bad person is someone who wants to do bad things."

"I don't understand exactly, but it sounds like what my counselor said to me."

"Tell me about it."

"Well, finally in ninth grade the school insisted I see a counselor because I was in trouble so much. I really liked him—"

"Sorry to butt in. Why did you like him?"

"Hmm. He was safe, you know. I didn't feel like he was going to start off telling me what to do. He listened."

"Good. Go ahead."

"Well, in time he suggested I get some testing done by a specialist."

"A doctor."

"I guess so."

"And your mother agreed with this?"

"Yes. The counselor went and talked to her. I think she was getting pretty desperate too."

"What happened then?"

"The doctor prescribed some medicines."

"Do you know what they were?"

"Can't remember."

"Are you taking meds now?"

"Oh, sure. They've changed, but I'm still taking them. I take four Wellbutrin each day [400 milligrams] and Adderall. I took Ritalin for a while."

"James, can you compare the feelings you have now to those you had before you started counseling and medicine?"

"I can mostly remember the feelings before because they were all the way back to grade school. I think already then I felt like the oddball in the classroom. I felt that I just couldn't do the work. I basically gave up before I started. I always had that feeling. I couldn't keep up. The harder I tried, the more anxiety I had."

As he talked about his struggle, James grew increasingly more agitated. I wanted to keep him talking for a few more minutes. There was something undiscovered yet.

"How did you feel when you were diagnosed?"

"With ADD? Well, I was relieved in a way, but I was also discouraged. I figured if I had this, there's no hope for me."

"How do you deal with it?"

James thought for a while. "Maybe the biggest problem is the medicine. When I'm feeling pretty good, I don't want to take it. So I'll go for a week or so without it. Then if I get depressed or anxious, I take it again. I know I'm supposed to take it regularly, but I don't want to be dependent on medicine to be myself.

"Or else," he added, "I just forget to take doses. Then when

I miss, I figure, why worry? Then I miss the next dose too."

"Do you keep a planner?"

"Oh, yeah. My coach helps me with it every Monday morning."

"Do you follow it?"

"Sometimes."

When James left, he commented, "I hope I've been able to help you." I thanked him. But I was left wondering, who is going to help James?

I knew the answer. At this stage, only James can. He faces the frightening task of fully admitting to his illness. Perhaps his mother's denial during his youth has colored James' denial. James has to admit, furthermore, that he needs help for his illness—that there is medical and therapeutic help available, but that he has to own it. By that I mean that he has to accept and take charge of it.

James faces a rough road. My heart bleeds for him because he is several times a victim. He is the victim of an illness that he had nothing to do with, that is not his fault, and that he certainly did not wish for. Moreover, he is the victim of an early childhood in which his illness was denied and help refused. Finally, James is his own victim. He himself has not fully admitted to his illness and has denied the help, pharmaceutical and therapeutic, available to him.

The cases that we have examined in this chapter outline the most immediate solutions to living with ADHD.

- First, we recognize that ADHD is a disorder that cannot be cured but *can be managed.*

- Second, we realize that *family support* is a crucial element in the management process.
- Third, we understand the full and necessary role of *specialized medical care* in the form of testing, evaluation, and diagnosis.
- Fourth, we recognize the important role of *pharmaceutical intervention* and the careful role of *coaching, planning, and organization.*

We turn next, then, to several broader solutions to living, and living happily and successfully, with ADHD.

FIVE

A Brief Word on Children, Adult Women and Men, and Other Strange Species of the Human Race

Sometimes when the pollen is heavy in the air, we have to clear our sinuses.

We talked earlier about ADHD myths. This is a good point to pause and clear out some of the smaller details—those microscopic bits of pollen—that can make a life miserable.

Bad Boys and Dreamy Girls

ADHD affects approximately 5 percent of school-age children. The number doesn't sound too bad until you consider that it represents several million children. That makes ADHD the most common mental disorder among children.

But wait. Generally, ADHD is diagnosed three to four times more frequently in boys than in girls. Is it something intrinsic to male biology that leads to their more frequent diagnosis?

Not necessarily. For a while people were raising a ruckus, saying that Ritalin and other stimulants were prescribed too often in the U.S. In fact, the U.S. medical and research professions have developed and provided the best diagnostic tools. Many from this professional community stress that ADHD is still *underdiagnosed.* Too many children are suffering needlessly.

This may be especially true of school-age girls. Some studies have suggested that girls are more prone to ADHD—*primarily inattentive.* They're "dreamy," not rambunctious. They would rather escape to their make-believe world than try to live in the real world.

The evidence suggests that these young girls often suffer the psychological effects of their ADHD. They don't want to participate in after-school activities. They feel lonely and left out. Often academic performance is affected. They just don't seem very bright.

Don't misunderstand the point here. Our schools and our children will always range across the intellectual spectrum. Different gifts will emerge. There is no magic pill to suddenly turn them all into world-class neurosurgeons. Nor would we want that *Brave New World* intrusion in our lives.

God has mysteriously crafted each one of us—before we ever appeared in our mothers' wombs—to be the people we are today. Teachers should look out over the classroom and see a glorious rainbow of gifts, of needs, of personalities and potentialities. But if she or he, looking out, begins to detect the little girl who is withdrawn, anxious, slow to do her homework, and a bit dreamy, then perhaps that teacher is also looking at a responsibility to be aware of potential need. Teachers are often the first line of defense in detecting ADHD among our children.

Little Children and Bad Events

When we talk about the effects of ADHD on children, however, we should also recognize some distinctions. ADHD is a medical condition. Behavioral problems among children that are caused by upsetting events are not necessarily signs of ADHD. They may be attributable to the events themselves. For example, if a child has witnessed a terrible accident, the vivid memory may live on for weeks or months after the event. The child may show signs of inattention, distractibility, and withdrawal commonly associated with ADHD.

Similarly, emotional stress or trauma can create symptoms associated with ADHD. Notoriously difficult on children are the processes of divorce, a death in the family, moving, and changing schools. Each of these generates strong and compelling mood shifts that the child is not psychologically equipped to handle. Consequently the child "acts out" the emotional turmoil. He or she may pick fights at school or give up on schoolwork. The emotions may surface in anger, impulsively directed at authority figures. The child might try to hide from these emotions by constant activity resembling hyperactivity.

In such instances children may exhibit symptoms common to an ADHD diagnosis yet not have the medical condition. This is one reason why the *DSM-IV* criteria call for persistence of symptoms, as we saw in the previous chapter.

Hearing, Not Listening

Quite often ADHD children get confused about what they are supposed to do in school assignments. They have missed parts of the instructions. At other times they may know what to do, but because of the accelerated rush of ideas in their brains, they do not consistently do what they know to do.

One can almost follow a progression of this basic trait through childhood. In the earliest stages the child simply fails to pay attention to details. He never seems to notice that his room resembles the aftermath of a hurricane. He can still find his bed. She isn't bothered by the fact that she put on two different socks. In first grade neither of them pays attention to the math problems at the bottom of the page. They solved the top ones. Now it's time to doodle. She wants to draw a picture of the back of Margaret's head. He draws Super Mario crunching through a tunnel.

As such children grow older, they sort of flit around social groups like bewildered moths. They don't quite seem to fit in. But they are also in constant motion when they play by themselves. They might move from toy to toy, then finally just kick all the toys out of the way in frustration.

One father told me that he was amazed by what happened when his seven-year-old ADHD son pulled a big box of Legos from the toy closet one Saturday morning. The boy took a brief break for lunch, but then he worked steadily (hyperfocus) on his structure until 5:00 P.M., when his parents got him to come to dinner. At first he explained what he had built. Then the whole subject just left his mind. He never looked at the structure again, even though his parents left it up for a week. Lack of focus or hyperfocus—it can change from day to day.

As a child moves through the grades, the more classic symptoms of ADHD emerge. He or she might sit in the classroom, and even have eye-to-eye contact with the teacher, yet have no clue what was said. It's the old hear-but-not-listen routine. Suddenly ten minutes' worth of homework takes several hours because the child keeps slipping away.[1]

Here's Mom Joan, who has seated her daughter Jaime at the kitchen table after school to do her homework. Joan knows she won't have a chance after supper because then Jaime will be off in her own world altogether. She looks at ten-year-old Jaime's homework and thinks, *With any luck, this can't take more than fifteen minutes.*

Jaime sits at the table. She glances at the homework.

"I can't do it, Mom."

"What do you mean?"

"I mean I don't understand it."

"Didn't the teacher give directions?"

"She never does."

"Well," Joan asks, trying another tactic, "you want to pass the course, don't you? I mean, you don't want to take it all over again."

"I don't care. It's all stupid anyway."

"Here. Let me help you with the first one. Hmm. 'Circle the main verb of the sentence.' That shouldn't be hard. What's a verb?"

"I don't know. She never told us."

"Well, I bet you have a definition in your notes."

Of course there's no definition in Jaime's notes. After Joan helps her with the first problem, circling the verb, boxing the subject, underlining nouns and pronouns, she tells Jaime to stay at the table until she gets them finished.

A half hour passes. It's quiet. *Too* quiet.

When Joan checks on her, Jaime is staring out the kitchen window, chewing on the end of her pencil. And how many more problems has she done? You're right. None.

During the elementary grades the academic problems associated with ADHD first become pronounced. It may be Jaime's hearing-versus-listening syndrome. Oddly enough, the ticking of a distant clock can be enough to drive Jaime to distraction. Her symptoms often appear in her inability or disinclination to finish homework or school projects. Chores get half-done or ignored altogether. *Organization* is a word spoken on Jupiter. And lose things! Just name it—pens, pencils, backpacks, lunches, sports items—the list keeps going.

ADHD children who incline toward pronounced hyperactivity and impulsivity experience other emerging symptoms. You can spot him in the classroom. He fidgets, squirming restlessly in his seat, constantly shifting positions. He hops all over the place in play activities. In the classroom he often talks excessively, sometimes blurting out answers to the teacher's question before it is completed. And then the answer often has very little to do with the question. Just a random thought. He butts into conversations and has trouble waiting his turn.

When he comes home, he barges in the back door like a cyclone. "I hate school," he announces. He scrounges in the refrigerator, leaves orange peelings on a shelf. The backpack lies in the middle of the kitchen floor, the coat thrown into the dining room. After fifteen or twenty minutes he says, "I'm bored. There's never anything to do around here." He has three friends his age in the neighborhood, but he's waiting for *them* to call *him.*

Will They Ever Grow Up?

The greater freedom and individuality that high school affords affect the ADHD teen in several ways. On the positive side, the resources in high school are generally greater than in the lower grades. Resource rooms, counselors, and tutors are common at many, if not most, American high schools.

At the same time, high school represents that great coming-of-age event, the driver's license, and more unstructured free time and more avenues of individual expression. While many of these are relatively harmless (a teenager needs a car to get to work), and while many can positively reinforce responsibility (having a job), any freedom involves risks. So it was in Eden. So it is with the descendents of Adam and Eve today.

Coexisting Conditions

During the high school years in particular, certain conditions that frequently coexist with ADHD (comorbidity) may appear. Recent studies have mapped the presence of other coexisting disorders as well. Most commonly, ADHD is found to coexist with depression and anxiety, but more recently ADHD has been linked in comorbidity with Tourette's Syndrome and Obsessive-Compulsive Disorder.

Another area under scrutiny is the relationship of Oppositional-Defiant Disorder and ADHD. In particular, the impulsivity characteristic of ADHD seems to drive the ODD. The child lashes out in anger, cannot see things in any way but his or her own way, and defies any suggestions of compromising actions (including counseling).

The study of ADHD and comorbidity has produced widely fluctuating figures, demonstrating that the work is hardly conclusive yet. For example, a CHADD (Children and Adults with Attention-Deficit/Hyperactivity Disorder) Fact Sheet (2000) states that approximately 40 percent of ADHD patients have oppositional-defiant disorder. Conduct disorder occurs in 25 percent of children, 45 to 50 percent of adolescents, and 20 to 25 percent of adults. CHADD figures suggest that 10 to 30 percent of children and 47 percent of adults experience comorbidity with depression. About 20 percent manifest bipolar disorder. About 30 percent of children and 25 to 40 percent of adults have an anxiety disorder. In addition, CHADD points out that adolescents are at increased risk for cigarette, alcohol, and drug abuse—in that order of progression.[2]

All Grown Up

Whether one takes the conservative figures or the more expansive figures, the scenario of comorbidity is scary. Raising a teenager is hard enough in the best of times. These sound like impossible times!

Mark Twain once said about teenagers that when they turn thirteen, you put them in a barrel with a hole in it to feed them. Then when they turn sixteen you plug the hole. I trust no one is frightened to that extent, nor should we be. A hundred years after Mark Twain we live in an age of far greater medical, diagnostic, and treatment skills.

The other issue we have to consider here is ADHD among adults, and particularly those little girls we looked at earlier. Suddenly they're all grown-up women, right? And they grew right out of their ADHD and lived happily ever after. For a long time people believed the fairy tale. It was how we were supposed to think. You're a grown-up now. Act like it. How nice it would be if we could step away from ADHD, say, on our twenty-first birthday. That's a good day to be grown up now.

The fact is that some children *do* seem to outgrow ADHD. Intuitively or by counseling, they learn coping mechanisms that permit them to function just fine. For many others, however, the coping mechanisms seem like bars on the tiger of ADHD that lurks within, producing a constant anxiety over the ferocity of the beast. Sometimes these are the "driven" people, often excelling dramatically in their positions. Sometimes they are the people that crash into the tiger's cage. One CHADD Fact Sheet states that

> Contemporary research has shown that up to 70 percent of children diagnosed with AD/HD will continue to have symptoms of the disorder that significantly interfere with academic, vocational, or social functioning in their adult lives. AD/HD in adults is sometimes viewed as a "hidden disorder" because the symptoms of AD/HD are often obscured by problems with relationships, organization, mood disorders, substance abuse, employment, or other psychological difficulties.[3]

The percentages vary from study to study because, in contrast to the situation in childhood diagnosis, a standardized set of criteria specifically for adults is not available.

But what about those little girls who have grown up to be adult women, sometimes with little girls of their own? Medical attention has increasingly turned to them.

The evidence of genetic influence on ADHD indicates that the incidence of ADHD among girls may have been understated and underdiagnosed. Using those genetic clues, professionals are discovering that 50 to 60 percent of ADHD cases persisting into adulthood are among women. And this finding is getting publicity. Recently, *Time* magazine ran a story entitled "Ritalin: Mom's Little Helper."[4] In a study published in 1997 in the *Journal of Attention Disorders* on the psychological functioning of ADHD women, the authors found a higher incidence of depressive episodes, lower self-esteem, more anxiety, and the feeling of less control over their lives.[5]

ADHD was for a long period misdiagnosed, underdiagnosed, and misunderstood among children. It has, fortunately, now come out of the closet of dark little secrets, and millions of children benefit from treatment. For many adults, however, ADHD hides under a series of masks and props the adult casts over his or her life. The hyperactivity may be funneled into a ceaseless series of tasks that drive a person to the point of collapse. Inability to focus can hold one back in the work force or impair daily life in innumerable ways. Impulsivity, particularly if paired with a coexisting condition like bipolar disorder, can lead one into serious lapses in judgment—and serious consequences.

If ADHD is an issue of great concern for our children, in

many ways it is even more so for us adults, where it has been so profoundly underdiagnosed until the last decade. In many respects we still carry all the stigma of children a generation or two ago. "They just can't cut it." "A bad person." And so on. As with those children, recognition, diagnosis, and treatment are the beginning steps to restored psychological health.

SIX

Finding Real Solutions: Discipline in the Home

The very first step toward real solutions for living with ADHD has been covered in the previous chapters. A great deal of confusion and misunderstanding still persists about the disorder. The first solution, then, is to form a careful understanding of the illness itself. We who live with ADHD, either as family members or by having the disorder ourselves, need to know what the clinical parameters of the disorder are, what the experience is like, and what some of the standard treatments are. In addition, however, a number of solutions to living with ADHD have proven helpful.

But pause a minute and reflect on what we have to deal with. Our concerns are not only with our immediate family but also with society. Imagine the family that lives up the block. You can picture them. You can name them. They seem swaddled in success. They define the American dream and rest comfortably in spiritual order. Nothing impugns their bright and shining name or their orderly lives. It seems their very house bespeaks prosperity. Every year or so they undertake some remodeling or expansion project. Their underground sprinkling never leaks. They don't even have moles in their yard. They lease two new cars every two years—his and her models of the same make. He has twice served as an elder on the church council. She is currently a deacon.

Their two children testify to their success. The older, Joshua, is in his last year of dental school. He has recently become engaged to his college sweetheart. And June—why, after four years as an honors student in college, she had her pick of law schools. But she picked one in state so she could be near her family. What wonderful children! What wonderful parents!

Of course they are. But now confess to a bit of envy, or maybe just a hint of resentment. Sure, you could lease new cars, but you're paying off the medical bills that your insurance doesn't cover. Two of your three children have ADHD, and this in turn led to Dad's diagnosis of ADHD. Three people in a household of five! Sometimes it seems like an absolute zoo in your house. Someone is always on edge or off the edge. Someone wanders off right at dinner time, ("Oh, I wasn't hungry yet.").

Then there's that hole in the hallway. When Jonathan was being disciplined by being sent to his room, he impulsively turned and kicked at the wall. ("I didn't mean to break it.") The hole is about a foot across. Dad keeps promising to fix it on Saturday, but Saturdays come and go, and he's always busy with some other project. His line: "This will only take an hour. Then I'll get to the wall." Problem is, the projects never get done in an hour; other things intervene. After all, the car does have to get washed. And the yard should be mowed.

Chaos and disorder. Let's take these kids and put them out at the corner with big signs around their necks: *Free to Good Home*. Better yet, scratch out *Good Home*.

What terrible children! What perfectly awful parents!

So we often feel about ourselves. And it doesn't really help very much to tell ourselves that ADHD is definitely *not* the result of bad parenting. It is a disorder in brain chemistry. That wouldn't change if the child in question were a son or daughter of the President and First Lady.

But the first very real and most demanding challenge to parents of ADHD children is the whole issue of discipline. Granted, our children may never be the ideally behaved Joshua and June. (Go ahead and have a moment of resentment. It's okay.) But there are certain measures of discipline and direction that can work toward solutions. Remember, however, that by talking about "Real Solutions," we are talking about *living with the disorder*. We want to ease the burden, for we know we can't wave some magic wand and have it go away.

Planning Discipline

As parents, our approach to discipline is generally reactive. We set in place what we consider to be thoroughly fair and specific rules for our children. If a child has the audacity to break one of our well-reasoned rules, and to defy our authority to impose them, we react with what we consider reasonable discipline.

We know it doesn't work that way with ADHD children. Their brains seldom permit the strategically "reasonable" analysis of actions and consequences. Instead of simply establishing rules of conduct, essential as they are, we also have to establish a *plan for dealing with misconduct*.

Two essential elements have to precede our plan. First, we cannot forget that our child has an illness. I would *never* advocate pointing this out to the child during discipline. It tears self-esteem to shreds. It makes the child angry, defiant, and rebellious. He or she is well aware of the fact. But it is something that we as parents have to remind ourselves when we discipline. Consequently, and secondly, our discipline has to be grounded in love, firmness, and consistency.

Those qualities have to guide our discipline plan. If we as parents have them firmly embedded in our minds, they give us greater confidence that what we are doing is right. You see, the one thing we have to try to avoid is responding to an angry and disoriented child in a like manner. It is important to be able to remain calm and firm in the face of anger. Often, we remember, the child will feel that he or she does not need discipline.

One of the most effective tools for discipline is the "One-Two-Three-Magic Plan," pioneered by T.W. Phelan.[1] This plan should be carefully explained to the child. When Pat and I have used it, we have written all the steps down, explained them precisely, and kept the written list in a readily accessible place—a kitchen cupboard, in our case. The stages are these:

1. Making direct eye contact with the child, Mom or Dad holds up one finger. This level means, "Stop the words!" Stop talking, arguing, or whatever. In this way the parent recognizes the objectionable behavior and tells the child to disengage from it.

2. Direct action. Here you tell the child, if he or she persists in the objectionable behavior, "Jerome, you were just given a warning and you did not stop. Now we are at level two. You have a choice. You can go to your

room for fifteen minutes. Or you can go downstairs and punch the boxing bag for ten minutes, or you can walk the dog around the block." The idea here is to remove the child from the scene or to get him engaged in some physical activity that will vent the emotions.

3. If the child still does not follow through, tell him that he must go to his room for an hour and stay there. Don't expect him simply to disengage without protest. Be prepared to wait a few minutes, but be firm. Permit reading materials in his room. The point is to defuse. Never seize the child to force him into his room. This will only fuel the situation and also make the parents feel angrier.

In the presence of ADHD all discipline is strictly hands off. This is largely a self-protective measure for parents. The legal system in America now gives nearly 100 percent credibility to the child. Say that your child makes an off-hand passing remark to his gym teacher, "My dad grabbed me last night." The child says it impulsively. He isn't thinking about the consequences. But the gym teacher is required by law to report anything he suspects as abuse. What does "grabbing" mean? And so the police pick up Dad, and at best, he will spend a day or two in jail, until he can hire an attorney and have a court date set.

We have to examine some contingencies here, but for a moment let's assume the best. The child accepts the discipline and afterward feels contrition. We have a long-standing rule in our family that whenever one person says, "I'm sorry," the other person must immediately say, "I forgive you." No harumphing, no hemming or hawing, no disgruntled talk. Only an immediate, unqualified "I forgive you."

But with ADHD we find the need for further affirmation. Parents should add something like, "Jerome, we love you very much. We need obedience and cooperation in our home. We are your parents, and we have to control what happens in our home. This is what a Christian family is about. This is fair to you and us. We want to help you learn self-control so you can feel safe in our home too."

In fact, parents of ADHD children should be on constant lookout for moments to praise and affirm their child's ability and work. Consider mailing a card with a personal note to your child. Take him or her out for some personal time doing something the *child wants to do*. Praise a school project as if it were the only one on earth. Praise always extends farther than the fence of discipline.

Emotional Escalation

We like to assume restoration similar to that just described, and sometimes it does go that way. Sometimes, however, it goes from bad to worse. The child's tensions escalate. So too for the parents. What contingencies come into play then?

Before we leap to any conclusions here, however, we should remind ourselves not to play psychiatrist with our own children. Emotional outbursts may involve any of a wide range of behaviors, from typical childhood tantrums or teenage rebellion to those that indicate some specific disorder. If we expect the "normal" child to be a docile little figure, one who memorizes the Bible—and some passages backwards—and masters Einstein's theory by age four, we're in for a rude surprise. The best advice to any parent is, remember yourself as a child.

Furthermore, we should be realistic enough to bear in mind our earlier discussion that certain "comorbidities" frequently exist along with ADHD. Oppositional-defiant, obsessional-compulsive, and bipolar disorders—any of these may be lurking just under the ADHD symptoms. It is a task of the psychiatrist, of course, to make the observations that will reveal any coexisting disorders. And he or she has specific guidelines to help in diagnosis.

Recognizing that reality, we have to adjust the nature of the child's discipline to the nature of the illness. With those cautions, the following contingency actions might apply for those times when all our efforts to control actions and emotions (discipline) crumple like a straw house under the giant's foot.

1. *Keep in regular touch with your child's doctor (psychiatrist).* Keep him or her informed of behavior patterns, often calculated on a daily graph or in carefully kept notes. Don't try to rely upon memory alone. Quite often the child's more aggressive mood disorders can be modulated by fine-tuning both the type and amount of medicine. For example, Risperdal, originally used as an antipsychotic, has been very successful in controlling outbursts of anger and violent rages. As with the use of any drug, ask yourself the question: Is my child better off in the torment of this present condition or with a medicine that can greatly alleviate it?

2. *Never make a threat you're not willing to carry out.* Don't tell a twelve-year-old you'll call the police if you won't follow through on it. Scare tactics don't work, and the child will see right through them, simply bolstering his or her aggressiveness. But you do have options.

3. *Remove yourself.* That's right, get in the car and take a long drive. Try to quiet your pounding heart by taking a walk. Go out for dinner. Admittedly there are risks to this action, and surely they depend upon the age of the child. One would not, for example, want to leave the house and leave a preteen behind. Even a teenager, moreover, might chase you, banging on your car and screaming as you drive down the driveway. You might come back to find something in your house destroyed. Depending upon your view of the situation, it might be best simply to spend some time outside in close proximity to your house. Here you are in a "social" setting but outside the house. The point is that if your child refuses to disengage, you might have to disengage yourself. The parent of an ADHD child also has to be very careful to protect him- or herself.

4. *If the child gets physical, have one trusted friend—or neighbor, or pastor—who is aware of the situation and can quickly come over and intervene.* The person need not be an expert, only present. Quite often the simple presence of another person can defuse an explosive situation.

5. *When do you call the police?* Under three conditions:

- when the child is a danger to him- or herself
- when the child is a danger to the parent—physical-abusing or threatening with an object (knife, bat)
- when the child is on a destructive rampage—destroying furniture, breaking windows, etc.

Be prepared for the consequences. Rarely do police departments do counseling intervention anymore. Often they will be compelled to handcuff the child and remand him to juvenile court. The court can then place him or her under psychiatric care for a period generally ranging from forty-eight to seventy-two hours. If your child is already under psychiatric care, tell the police dispatcher that with your initial call. You should have plans for a specific hospital, arranged with the child's psychiatrist in advance. The police can escort the child to that psychiatric hospital with the cooperation of the psychiatrist. There the child will be remanded to the care of your doctor, who will lead the professional team at the hospital for as long as the child needs that care.

These measures range over a broad set of responses to a broad set of behaviors. The key is to have a plan in place and have the child fully aware of it. This holds true for more routine disciplinary matters also.

For example, the ADHD child's tendency to blurt out answers in the classroom might transfer to the home—but in this case by using inappropriate language. We keep a list of unacceptable words in our home. A violation requires writing lines such as "I will talk respectfully," or "I will use acceptable language." All the lines should be stated with positive verbs.

Finally, don't sweat the small stuff. Something about the mystery of adolescence suddenly makes a child incapable of turning off lights or shutting doors or the like. Sometimes the entire second floor is lit up and no one is up there. But you know who just was. It's not worth making a scene over. Tell yourself the exercise of climbing the stairs will do you good.

Our point in discipline is not to produce a perfect child. Such a creature doesn't really exist. Our aim is to manage according to plan so that we aren't swept away by the disruptive emotions of the illness.

In forming and in implementing that plan, both parents must be in complete agreement and completely consistent. Any teenager—especially a teenager with ADHD—will attempt to play one parent off another, seeking a dividing edge. Often he or she will alter the words or message of one parent. "But Dad said that...." They seem intuitively to know the old battle plan of divide and conquer. It's a power game. What the parents cannot do is give in to it. Absolute firmness and absolute unity are the keys to surviving as a family.

What's a Parent to Do?

Discipline, we recognize, is first and foremost a family affair. It is a biblical mandate for loving parents to exercise loving discipline. Loving discipline simply means that we acknowledge and try to prevent the wrong done, but that we steadfastly, without wavering, love the child who has done wrong.

Two qualifications enter into this matter of discipline.

Not a Solo Job
That it is first and foremost a family affair, exercised communally and in agreement by both parents, does not mean that those parents are isolated from other communities of help.

Parents of ADHD children overextend themselves. They see themselves as the frontline and the rear guard in the battle to discipline. They have to watch out for *themselves*, particularly in the sustained high-stress parenting required by an ADHD child.

Discipline is a joint task of school and parents. Just as the parents can't simply ignore the problem, neither can the school. Parents should be in contact with school authorities on discipline issues.

Parents have to make space for their marriage too. To protect and preserve their own marriage, they have to find their own space to reaffirm each other. They need an evening out for dinner and bowling or a movie. To do this they have to be willing to trust their child to a competent, older babysitter and *forget about it.* Give the sitter combat pay if necessary, but get out of there. Remember, your marriage was there before the child. Recall all the reasons why it came to be a marriage.

I also advocate getting an adult friend or relative to come into the home for a couple of days while the parents take an "overnighter" out of town. Try not to touch the phone to check in. They can reach you in an emergency. Take along books and magazines. Sit in the hot tub. Get the best room and dinner you can afford. You're worth every penny. And so is your marriage.

Grace and Consequences

The second qualification on our comments about discipline is harder to make. When do you let the child go? In a sense you never do. You never give up on the child or on God's grace. We need constantly to remind ourselves of the promises and power of that grace.

Indeed, Scripture provides a nearly seamless litany testifying to God's holding on to those whom he loves and those whom we have dedicated to him. In 1 Chronicles 17:13, where Nathan is testifying to God's grace toward David, the prophet declares, "I will be his father, and he will be my son. I will never take my love away from him...."

From our perspective, God had plenty of cause to remove his love from David, but God says he will *never* do so. These are words to set in our hearts when all seems to be going wrong, when all things in this life seem to be whirling out of our control.

At the end of his gospel, John writes that "Jesus did many other things as well. If every one of them were written down, I suppose that even the whole world would not have room for the books that would be written" (21:25). What things? All those things of Jesus' grace. But the center point of that grace, and the central testimony of John's gospel, is the grace of the cross, which defeats any power of evil and any shade of darkness.

We need to cling to such verses of courage when our best efforts at discipline seem to fail altogether. The reality that faces parents of ADHD children as they enter their later teenage years is that these children seem particularly prone to the temptations of this world. All the boundaries of discipline and moral behavior we worked so hard to establish seem to crumble to pebbles on the path to destruction. We might tell ourselves that the very impulsivity of the illness is to blame, but bad things are being done.

Again, what things? ADHD children are often prone to self-medicate themselves. It becomes a vicious cycle. They might try alcohol or marijuana to "take the edge off." When the inevitable rebound effect of depression occurs, they have to return again to their "relaxer." The cycle deepens. One night they're arrested for drunk driving. You get a call at 1:00 A.M. from the jail. What then?

There is always the matter of forgiveness and grace—but also consequences. If the child is arrested, the fine is his to pay. He's responsible, not you. He is making his choices as a young adult now. But you do insist upon certain rules of behavior and rules of the home. The rules of behavior include counseling for drug abuse, or whatever the act might be. It might involve mandatory sessions at Salvation Army alcohol counseling—a more spiritual and just as effective alternative to A.A. House rules might include:

- deadlines for being in on weekdays and weekends
- breath checks for alcohol, or eye checks for marijuana
- absolutely no prohibited substances in the house

If any of these are violated, the parents must have a firm course of action in mind. If the child is of majority (eighteen), you have the right to remove him from the home. This is a serious matter, but so too is your home. By the way, it is thoroughly hypocritical for parents to have alcohol in their home when a child is struggling with the addiction. Get rid of it. *All* of it.

These admittedly hard words need to be written; they arise from the reality of what some ADHD children fall prey to in their later teens. Don't make threats you are not willing to keep; be prepared beforehand with a plan to enact.

I am thinking of a couple whom I'll call Bruce and Linda, faced with this very challenge. Their son Robert had his first run-in with alcohol at seventeen when a neighbor called about a noisy party at a friend's house. Robert was charged with underage drinking. Before his eighteenth birthday, Linda found a bottle of rum behind the books on Robert's shelf while she was dusting. When Bruce and Linda confronted him, he said he was keeping it for a friend of his.

He was just nineteen, a part-time college freshman and working as a gardener, when he had his accident. Two-thirty in the morning. He didn't see the red light. Nor the car stopped in front of it. He rear-ended the car and virtually demolished his own. Robert called Bruce and Linda from the jail to bail him out. They refused. "We're sorry, Robert. You brought this on yourself, not us. You're going to have to deal with it." Two days later Robert finally got before a judge and was released on his own recognizance.

Bruce and Linda were faced with a hard decision. But they had prepared for it. They paid the first two months' rent on a room at a boarding house (the local YMCA was full). When they picked up Robert from jail, they returned home, packed all of Robert's things, and brought him to his new room. Surely there was anger, especially from Robert. "What! You're just kicking me out? What kind of parents are you?"

"We're parents who love you, Robert. And we'll always be there when you need to talk to us. But we can't support your behavior by letting you live in our home."

Bruce and Linda did this quickly, even if with hurting hearts. They had their plan in place. They did not have to tear themselves apart wondering if they were forsaking Robert. They were letting go, but also giving him up to God's care.

That wasn't the end of the matter for Bruce and Linda, however. Two realizations struck them. First, they needed help. Second, there must be other parents out there struggling with the same issues. The first step they took was to ask their pastor if there were any other parents he knew who were in similar situations, and, if so, to contact them about their interest in starting a prayer and support group. Two other couples responded. Wanting to broaden their base so it wasn't just an in-house group, they located two more couples from other churches.

They have met for three years now, bringing concerns and spending time in prayer over them. Although they keep their meetings fully private in a church room on a Sunday evening, they have shared so much that they now often do social things also—going out to dinner, meeting at one member's cottage, and the like.

We parents need support wholly as much as our children. It is far too easy to give them 100 percent of our attention. We also have to pay attention to ourselves. That, in itself, is a good and necessary spiritual discipline.

SEVEN

Real Solutions in Society:
Structure and Space

In the previous chapter we discussed real solutions for living with an ADHD child in the home. Although ADHD children are often disruptive or belligerent in school, they may also be able to bottle up their impulses in the social order of the schoolroom. When they come home, all restraints fall away the minute they step off the bus. The transformation is hard to believe as they enter their "safe" place. There's only Mom and Dad or a random sibling to vent on. The cork pops on the bottle, and potential explosions wait at every turn.

That is why most of the discussion on discipline in the previous chapter focused on home situations. The home must indeed be a safe place, but it must be safe for all its inhabitants. Therefore a discipline plan must be in place and enacted. Home life, especially with the ADHD child, needs structure. That is the case in society also.

In *It's Nobody's Fault*, Harold S. Koplewicz argues that "our lives are basically divided into three spheres: love, fun, and work. In the case of children, those spheres are translated into the relationship with their parents, social interactions with their friends, and learning in school."[1]

It's an interesting division, but it needs expansion. First, the triad of spheres that Koplewicz mentions doesn't stop at childhood. Given the fact that some 50 to 70 percent of childhood ADHD cases extend into adolescence, and that some of the remaining percentage have simply learned coping mechanisms and survival skills that permit them to live adequately with their disorder, it stands to reason that the three relationships will also extend into adulthood.

Second, Koplewicz's triad is incomplete because he has omitted the most significant relationship, that is, the spiritual one. So important do I believe that relationship to be in dealing with ADHD that I intend to examine it as a separate issue in a following chapter. At the moment, however, and taking our cue from Koplewicz's triad, consider several likely social difficulties and solutions to them.

Structure

Probably the most important solution to social problems arising from ADHD is structure. Remember that the ADHD brain reels back and forth from the edge of chaos. Lack of concentration to impulsivity to guilt to the tensions of trying to do better when you know you're going to fail again. The ADHD brain may be seen as a wild bronco kicking up its heels. The trick is not simply to rope the bronco and drag him into the corral. It will just keep smashing its heels against the rails. The trick is to make it at ease in the corral, to provide freedom to run out and stretch its legs but also to establish order in its daily habits.

Something of the same give-and-take applies to ADHD children and adults.

The Importance of Routine

One of the worst fears of ADHD children is losing control. They need routine. They panic when something significantly disturbs the routine. If she comes home from school expecting playtime and you announce that she has a dentist appointment instead, you have big trouble on your hands. One solution is preparation. Just how this should be done depends upon the age of the child. Young children (4-6) should be informed a day in advance about nonroutine events. Older children (7-12) should be informed a week in advance. Don't try to hold out long-term prospects. Generally the child's attention span can't encompass them.

Helping children cope with major breaks in routine. The exception to the above is for highly unusual events in which the child will be involved. Enlist him or her in the planning. For example, if your family is planning a spring trip to Florida, or to visit friends and relatives, involve the child in making choices. "Which toys would you like to take along?" "Which books?" "Why don't we make a list of things you're sure to want to take along?" Questions such as these prompt a child toward readiness, but they also let the child "own" the vacation. No longer seen as a disruption in the routine, he or she can now participate in it.

It may be that the child balks altogether at the change in routine. Moves to new locales and schools, for example, are particularly threatening and disorienting. Your wish is that your child adapt to the new locale as quickly as possible, of course, but ADHD children depend on routine and the patterns that mark the "normal" course of their lives; changes in those can create intense separation anxiety. What then?

Certainly, avoid threats like, "Well, we'll just have to leave you behind." This plays into the child's greatest fears. Instead, be intentional about doing some things that can help your child.

- First, insofar as possible, let the child participate in the plans. If you have purchased a new house, for example, take the child to see it. Let him or her get a feel for the house, particularly his or her new bedroom. Let the child participate in discussion of how the bedroom is to be decorated.
- Second, visit the new school the child will be attending. Do this after class hours. All the strange children milling about tend to reinforce the child's fear of the unknown. Walk through the school. Roam around the playground. Let the child get acquainted with the territory.
- Third, instead of just moving suddenly, help the child through the parting process itself. Throw a "goodbye" party—perhaps a sleepover with special friends. Take photographs of the "old house." Let your child prepare a scrapbook of favorite places.

Routine in adolescence. The need for routine patterns does not end with childhood. In adolescence the child acquires more independence and freedom of choice. The parents cannot impose a grid upon teens' lives. But they can help the adolescent with preparing a weekly planner. Be sure to include plenty of free time, and don't, by all means, try to fill up and account for every hour.

But significant events should be entered on the calendar.

What events? Most of them will involve school life:

- Monday: Outline for English paper. Do you have a topic?
- Tuesday: Study for biology test. Dentist appointment at 3:45.
- Wednesday: Biology test (use study hall and home on Tuesday for study).
- Thursday: Turn in outline for English paper. Do you have your topic? Out for dinner with Grandma.
- Friday: Half day of school. Take home the algebra textbook to work on problems.

The calendar doesn't have to be a whole lot more complicated than that. Some events, after all, routinely fall in place. The point is to highlight some areas that need particular focus. Notice the inclusion of dinner out with Grandma. That happens to be a weekly event in our family, but I include it here as a silent, positive incentive. Sometimes we tend to make the calendar so full of admonitions and exclamation marks that it only gets more confusing. It's a tool for guidance, not a command center.

Mentoring and Tutoring

Don't be surprised if your child adamantly resists mentoring or tutoring programs. Children don't want the stigma attached to them. They desperately want to be seen as "normal." Whatever that is, through adolescence it does *not* mean needing special help. Some parents might indeed find their child in such desperate academic situations that the child agrees to mentoring simply to survive. He or she also doesn't want to be seen as the "dummy." Other parents implement a reward system with the child, providing an outside incentive. Others simply leave the child to his or her own resources, feeling that they can't force the child to do the work.

Some try to help the child as best they can at home. We have found this the best alternative for us, although we have encouraged tutoring many times. We make ourselves available at study time to give what help we can. The only problem is, our help is limited. Mathematics, for example, has changed so dramatically since our own school days that it may as well be a foreign language. In our science classes we did lopsided experiments that stank up the room. Now young students are charting galaxies and breaking down DNA.

Tutoring and mentoring can be lifesavers for the academic health of ADHD children, but we need to differentiate between the two. A mentor is a model, an informal teacher, a friend and advocate. The idea of mentoring is to have an impartial, outside source in your child's life to give guidance. Most often, mentors are volunteers, perhaps through Big Brothers or Big Sisters programs or through nearby colleges. Their goal is to spend a regular amount of time on a regular basis with the child. Whether the time is dedicated to study or just having an outing, the goal is to develop a relationship with the child outside the home. This can also, by the way, give parents a wonderful break.

Mentors are also sometimes referred to as "coaches." As we saw in an earlier chapter, each of the ADHD students I interviewed had been assigned a coach. Their tasks were to help arrange a planner, mapping out the week's work, and to review grades and other marks of academic progress with the student. The mentor, or coach, fills a helping and trusting role.

A tutor has the highly specialized task of working through individual academic problems with a student. What kind of tutoring, or other academic help, is available depends upon the size and resources of a particular school. Tutors may be volunteers, or they may be specially trained teachers. Schools may offer only after-hours programs, or their main program may include resource centers and "parallel" classes, where the same subject is covered but in a smaller class and at a slower pace.

Legal Rights

Two federal laws—the Individuals With Disabilities Education Act (IDEA) and Section 504 of the Rehabilitation Act of 1973—have implications for children with ADHD. Both guarantee to children with disabilities a free and appropriate public education at the same level as that received by other children. Although more information may be obtained from one or more of the addresses and Web sites listed at the end of this book, several variations in the two programs may be listed briefly.

Who Is Covered?

IDEA requires that children have a disability requiring special education services. Section 504 applies when a child needs special education or related services. Typically, Section 504 covers those with less severe disabilities. Both laws apply to children diagnosed with ADHD.

Eligibility Criteria

Evaluation for IDEA, which generally provides full-time special education, examines the child's needs every three years. In the case of ADHD it must be demonstrated through professional diagnosis not only that the child has the disorder but also that the disorder directly interferes with the child's schoolwork. The school district is required to pay for that evaluation.

Evaluation for Section 504 generally has fewer restrictions than IDEA, but typically does require testing as part of an evaluation and implementation of a plan.

What Is Included?

IDEA provides what is called an Individualized Education Plan (IEP). In particular, IDEA performs what has been commonly called "mainstreaming." The child must be educated in the class he or she would be in without the disability. Special services are available to the child to enable him or her to perform successfully in that class.

Section 504 is generally more flexible, aiming to adapt solutions to the classroom the child would normally be in. In effect, Section 504 is a means to obtain assistance without the bureaucracy and paperwork of IDEA. IDEA, however, provides more intense, specialized educational treatment.

The information above is offered to acquaint you with the possibilities of additional, structured services for your child and shouldn't be taken as a legal directive. The point is that you do have rights. So does your child. Even if your child is in a parochial school, you can access these rights.

It may happen that, as you pursue such matters as these, you run into misunderstanding or simply get the runaround. Remember that *you are your child's advocate*. Teachers who properly understand the disorder can be of immediate and immense help. They perceive the need for structure in the workspace, the need for special testing places, and they also have the skill to weave these structures seamlessly into the fabric of the school day.

We happened to encounter one such particularly gifted teacher for one of our children. She had, first of all, the grace and perception to get to know each person in her class as a person. It was the proverbial "bad class." She had seven ADHD students out of approximately twenty-five—and possibly two or three more undiagnosed. Somehow she managed to be a calm presence in a storm of activity. *Activity* is the key word. She had the class working on projects nonstop to channel the energy. Creative projects. Research projects. Group projects. Seldom were the chairs in neat rows. Seldom did these kids learn as much in a year as they did in her class. The key was the fact that she knew the children's needs and capabilities, managing to focus upon both without letting one or the other become the defining factor for the child.

But such an intuitive and proactive understanding of children with ADHD, we must admit, is relatively rare. In its absence parents have to step in as advocates. Teachers may have to be informed, in complete confidentiality, of the child's needs. The same goes for school administrators. This process is not "making excuses"—dreaded words for the ADHD child. The parents may have to seek out help (IDEA or Section 504) beyond the classroom.

Space

The provision of space may seem like a contradiction to the provision of structure. Each, however, is necessary.

Persons with ADHD find it hard to focus on a structured sequence of events; therefore they need structure and routine provided. They find it nearly impossible to organize; therefore, they need the assistance of a planner. They crave social interaction and affirmation, but they often behave as bullies or test the limits of affirmation. Therefore they need guided or monitored social interaction.

But like all persons, they also need freedom to be themselves. We err if we try to *cage* ADHD persons in routines and structures. Providing space for the ADHD person consists of two primary factors. The first of these is to allow choices. Assuming an accountability system (discipline) and a directive structure system, it is possible nonetheless to grant the child sufficient freedom of choice that he or she feels responsible— less like a lab rat and more like a human.

Like so many things with this disorder, however, sometimes even the choices must be structured. Children (and adults) with ADHD tend to react impulsively, tossing reason aside like ribbons of confetti. If you have an ADHD teenager, for example, you might discover that he or she has filled out one of those ubiquitous mailers, *Get 12 CDs Free: only ten purchases over three years.* And there sits a big bill as your first awareness of it.

People with ADHD focus on what they want *now.* It nearly becomes an obsession for them. They can't hear any of your reasonable arguments why they shouldn't have it—either not now or never. In short, ADHD children can drown in a sea of open choices. Perhaps the worst thing parents can do is meet their every whim just to appease them, to stop the bickering, or to "avoid a scene." Real life won't be like that when they grow up.

But what is real life like? Real life, like the Christian life, assumes responsible freedom—choices within limits. The solution to training an ADHD child in this prospect is always to present choices within alternatives that you set. At the earliest stage of a child's life it may be setting alternatives for toy choices on a shopping trip. Surely the child may make up a birthday or Christmas list if you make it clear that you can't afford to buy everything on the list. Let the child occasionally select a restaurant for a family meal.

As the child grows into the trying teenage years, the structures may get harder to place as the teenager experiences greater independence. Still, they can be made. "You may have a sleepover on Friday night, but Saturday night will not work for us. Remember that you have to clean the family room after your guests leave on Saturday." Or, "You can cut the grass or wash the car on Saturday for your allowance"—or as part of required chores.

Besides choices, however, space also includes the simple matter of physical space. Children with ADHD need a spot in the house to call their own. For some it may be a certain chair in the living room for reading, certain untouchable areas of their bedroom for displays and collections, a section of the family room for such serious enterprises as building Lego cities or doing puzzles.

When my son was about five years old, we undertook a grand summer project of building together a clubhouse behind the garage. It was erected on solid 4x4 posts, six feet off the ground. We built a ladder to a hinged door and finished the clubhouse with plywood and a slanted roof. It had one hinged window at the end. We found scraps of carpet and glued them to the floor.

It was a truly grand place. And the neighborhood posse had a grand time there. They hung hooks and special objects (ropes, a hammer, a canvas nail bag, etc.) from the interior studs. They decorated the walls with crayon and chalk. My flashlights disappeared into a secret corner.

But then they discovered that they could expand their space, not by going up or out but down. They shoveled aside the wood chips underneath and began digging holes. Truly majestic holes. The dirt had enough clay in it that I didn't have to worry about it caving in, even when the holes were deeper than their heads. For the next few years, until we finally had to tear the dilapidated clubhouse down, it was a scene of holes, with special rocks and debris hoarded like gold in the clubhouse. It was their space. Every child, and especially the ADHD child, needs one.

Space, however, extends beyond those familiar parameters of a territory we call our own. It also extends into society. Here space is a sense of feeling comfortable, and it takes on many forms. For some it may mean having a designated testing place free of distractions.

For me it is often a matter of planning ahead. For example, in church I have to sit at the end of a pew. It makes no particular difference what pew, just as long as it's the end. If I move in toward the center, claustrophobia begins to press on me like a weight. I need a means of exit, whether I use it or not. When I travel by plane, I routinely order a window seat. I can look out and pretend the cramped cabin isn't there. I have to take steps to narrow my focus, concentrate my energy. At the same time, I have to take daily steps, through exercise, to displace the physical energy that can well up in the ADHD person like a volcano.

And when those times come when none of the steps seem to help? When it seems I can't connect two thoughts or complete a coherent sentence? When focus fractures like images in a kaleidoscope? I'll be honest. I try to ride it through. I hold on tight to any point of balance (reading a book, for example) and pray that it will pass and that the medications that I take four times a day like a psychological offering will actually do their job. Then I am reminded that I'm managing this illness that I have—not trying to cure it.

EIGHT

Real Solutions in the Workplace

We don't remain children forever. We somehow make it through adolescence and grow into a career. And those of us who grew up with ADHD will very likely carry it right along with us.

There used to be a myth that one "grew out of" ADHD. Indeed, the authoritative *DSM-IV* focuses its criteria and discussion almost exclusively on childhood and the adolescent years. The point is well made because the symptoms of ADHD are most clearly observable during these years. The *DSM-IV* places two cautions upon diagnosis in adults. First, "Caution should be exercised in making the diagnosis of Attention-Deficit/Hyperactivity Disorder in adults solely on the basis of the adult's recall of being inattentive or hyperactive as a child, because the validity of such retrospective data is often unreliable."[1] The second caution is that, if the adult once had ADHD, it may now be labeled as "In Partial Remission." This diagnosis "applies to individuals who no longer have the full disorder but still retain some symptoms that cause functional impairment."[2]

This places us in that shady area between medicine as an art (perceptiveness and guesswork) and medicine as a science (exclusive reliance upon data). It is not altogether helpful for the ADHD adult. For example, one might not display all the symptoms, or even those of childhood, because one has intuitively adapted coping mechanisms. Nonetheless, recent medical research has clearly demonstrated the need for professional diagnosis of adults with ADHD, and pharmaceutical or counseling intervention or both. Proper diagnosis can relieve the frequent anxiety, low self-esteem, and social fears that afflict these adults.

The question here, however, is whether specific solutions, beyond recognition that one has the disorder, can help stabilize one's life in the workplace, home, and society. It would be remiss not to acknowledge Kathleen Nadeau's ground-breaking work in this area, *ADHD in the Workplace*.[3] Nadeau ably demonstrates career tracks that nicely match the unique gifts and challenges of an ADHD adult, analyzes workplace "traps," and provides many practical strategies for surviving in the workplace that I have adopted.

With the recommendation noted, consider the following survival tools for the workplace.

Learn the Art of Saying No

There is no harder lesson to learn. It heads the list. Being asked to do additional jobs, to chair committees, to speak here or lecture there boosts our self-esteem. We feel important and needed. My, after being asked to serve as a third-term elder or deacon, we feel like spiritual giants. Being asked to serve on that fourth charity board or committee makes us feel indispensable. Even our good deeds clutter our psyches. If you volunteer six hours a week at the homeless shelter, why not up it to ten, knowing how desperately short of help they are? Or why not add some time at the church food pantry? If you're already teaching Sunday school, surely you can teach Wednesday Bible study too.

We feel needed. We feel that things wouldn't succeed without us. And we feel as frazzled as an old blanket that's been through the wash too many times. Someone put me on the shelf and leave me there!

That "someone" is you.

While the urge to accept ever-new challenges satisfies the fundamental human desire for self-esteem, it also marks the impulsivity associated with ADHD. We leap into situations rather than studying them. Consequently, after the grand leap, we find ourselves in deep waters that threaten to engulf us. We recognize that many of these activities are good and necessary. We also recognize our limitations of engagement. Several steps help protect us.

Avoid Commitment Overload

One of the fundamental traits of ADHD is impulsivity. Therefore the fundamental safeguard is to place checks upon it. These guidelines help toward that end.

Plan ahead. Know what you and your schedule can bear. If asked to add things to your schedule, you can respond, "I'm sorry. I wish I could, but I'm already committed to _____ for the coming year."

Think it over. If the prospect is one that genuinely appeals to you, you might respond, "That sounds interesting. May I have a few days to think it over?" The guideline here is never to leap head foremost into a situation you haven't thought through and prayed over carefully.

Know your personal skills. If an inner-city mission is pleading for help but you are anxious and uncertain being there, perhaps you can find other places to employ your skills. For example, for years my wife, Pat, a nurse, volunteered at an inner-city clinic for the homeless. I'm not a nurse. I would just be in the way at the clinic. Instead, I volunteered during that time writing résumés for jobless veterans at a veterans' counseling center.

Keep a steady course. Once you plan your course of action, including your responsibilities to work and home, stick by it for the long haul. If a new job and locale look attractive, by all means investigate, but weigh the cost to yourself and your family. No amount of money replaces the luxury of a calm state of mind.

Govern Distractibility

The considerations listed above are intended as checks on impulsivity, which can lead to the deadening cycle of commitment overload. There are also steps to protect yourself directly at the workplace.

In 1994, Doctors Hallowell and Ratey published their work, *Driven to Distraction.* The title works two ways. Parents are often driven to distraction as they try to figure out and govern the rampant distractibility of their ADHD child. Persons with ADHD, moreover, are often driven by the distractibility characteristic of the disorder, leaving in their path a litter of wrong turns and crashes.

This same distractibility can raise its wayward course in the workplace. Like a governor on a car engine, certain steps are needed to govern distractibility.

Structure

In the same way that ADHD students, through college, need a planner to structure their day, so too does the ADHD person in the workplace. Don't allow things to just happen. Organize.

Keep a planner. The planner is still the most effective means to organization. Just as important as the things you do are the things you don't do. Make sure the planner includes strategic breaks, and *use* them. Arrange time to take a short walk during a break, away from the workplace. Many people keep a pair of walking shoes in a desk drawer for this very reason.

Break large tasks into segments. If you look at the necessary end product, it may indeed seem endless. But break it into chunks of time, creating manageable goals for each day or even part of the day.

For example, I keep a regular writing schedule of Tuesday and Thursday mornings, sometimes a couple of hours on Saturday. During that time I write for forty-five minutes, then take a fifteen-minute break. I go outside to work in the garden, walk the dog, or do some other physical activity. On an average day I write four to five pages (in longhand), sometimes up to seven. The point is that I have to focus on manageable segments so that I don't become distracted by the whole.

Work *and* Exercise

Maintain a regular exercise schedule. Before or after the day of work you need the feeling of a "clear head," a separateness through exercise that creates the transition between home life and workplace. Psychological journals overflow with articles that relate exercise to a quiet mind.

Office Arrangement

I use the term "office" here, although I believe the points can apply to a variety of workspaces.

The college where I work requires me to keep my office door open whenever I'm in it. It's a good requirement with which I heartily concur. Meeting that requirement *and* governing my distractibility has been a challenge, however. If I had my desk facing the door, I'd be glancing up every five seconds to see who was passing by. All my workspace, therefore, keeps my back toward the door. Moreover, I keep that workspace framed with some meaningful objects of home life: photos, cards, a few sentimental objects, and the like.

The same principle can be applied in a number of different workplace situations. The object is to enable yourself to focus on the job at hand.

Liberation From Technology

The modern workplace is often a laboratory of technology, all designed to get the job done faster, easier, and more nearly perfectly. We forget that very real persons are driving the technology. We are paid to drive the computer, answer and direct the phones, complete reports. This environment has the distractibility quotient of a three-ring circus. What to do?

Remember you're not a slave to the machine. Plan strategic breaks where you're doing "legwork" or some other physical task.

If possible, assert authority over the machinery according to your schedule. Too often my schedule upon arriving at the office runs like this: Check the phone for voice mail while switching the computer on. Take notes on the voice mail while I bring up e-mail on the screen. Read the e-mail while checking the daily schedule.

Simplify! I tell myself. Enjoy that cup of coffee while reflecting on the day's schedule. Ninety-five percent of the e-mail, I find, can be deleted. Some of it (like "Spam" or other advertising documents) can go without being read. And I make a list of the necessary things to do on that particular day, so that I don't come to the end of the day still faced with them. As Henry David Thoreau said in *Walden*, "Our lives get frittered away with detail."

Stopping the Itch

A number of other ADHD symptoms fester in the workplace to confound one's best efforts to complete the assigned task successfully. They seem like poison ivy, festering in spots here and there until finally the itch spreads all over. Relieving the itch is the only thing that matters. The larger task itself disappears. One needs psychological strategies to protect against the festering of certain ADHD problems.

The Memory Sieve

Two things happen to me with memory problems. First, I focus so hard on the thing(s) I think I have to remember that I forget several lesser items I have to take care of. Focusing on a large project, I forget the overdue library books lying by the desk. Or second, trying to take care of a backlog of "minor" things, I find myself buried in a litter of papers. Search as I might, there are items I can't find. I know I had them; what did I do with them?

Two solutions apply here. They also work together.

Keep a detailed agenda. I like calendars with big blocks of space so that I can get all the details—deadlines, appointments, etc.—right in front of me. I have to see how the week shapes up. I have to keep track of the books I loan out.

In a similar fashion, I have to stack library books that I have borrowed in a certain place, so I can keep track of them.

Employ a very simple but carefully arranged filing system. This surprisingly simple but effective strategy should include all household records: car titles, tax forms, insurance documents, and so forth. Ask yourself this: If I am incapacitated tomorrow, will someone be able to take over these affairs with clarity and purpose? I have to do the same with files at work. Instead of piling up papers on my desk, once a week I have to order them into well-labeled folders. Once a year I go through them and throw out all nonessentials.

When I have failed to use this system, I've found myself wasting an hour or more looking for a certain document.

Throw out what you don't absolutely need; carefully label and file everything you do need.

Interpersonal Relationships

Remember old Aunt Buttinski? You couldn't say a word when you were a kid because she'd interrupt with her opinion. Remember her to avoid being like her. It's still an irritating practice, even when we do it ourselves.

The trouble is, the pattern is common to ADHD, and it can indeed cause irritation with coworkers. The pattern takes three forms:

- carrying on *your* conversation without permitting others an opportunity
- interrupting the conversation of others with impulsive comments
- blurting out reactions that are too blunt and that could be more graciously stated with a moment's reflection

The protection is to tell yourself to pause a moment. If the comment is significant, it will also be so a minute or two later. If a flare of anger makes you want to tell someone off, *do* something before you act verbally. Take a moment to get a drink of water or have a cup of coffee. Ask yourself if there are alternate ways of dealing with the problem, whether you can delegate it or avoid it altogether.

The Downright Awful Bad Days

I wish everyone could learn this fact early in his or her working careers. It took me way too long. No person—not you, not anyone—is absolutely indispensable to the workplace.

If you have ADHD, you know that you'll have some days in the course of the year when your head is spinning, you can hardly concentrate enough to get dressed, and about all you can do is sit there and watch the clock hands move without even knowing what time it is.

Take the day off. Call in sick. Sick days are not just for broken legs; they are also for miswired brains. You'll tell yourself, "But I have to do this!" No. You don't. The world, believe it or not, will get by just fine.

You need quiet for healing. Maybe a ride to a lake or a park. Work in the garden. Go for a bicycle ride. Admit to yourself that you need the healing.

The workplace can be a trying place for anyone and a pure trial for ADHD persons. In *Ordering Your Private World*,[4] Gordon MacDonald provides what I have long considered one of the most useful guides to living with ADHD, even though it doesn't mention the disorder once. MacDonald makes a clear distinction between being a "*driven* people" and "*called* people." Driven people, he points out, are blown about by winds of change and demands. They are victims of expectations that they can't fully direct or meet. Called people come to an understanding of who they are in this world of demands and change.

On the one hand, for our purposes, that means learning the artistry of a gracious "no" to those demands and a clear sense of abilities and limitations. On the other hand, however, it necessitates a clear understanding of ourselves as a people called by God—our spiritual place in the world. That issue is the subject of the next chapter.

NINE

Spiritual Solutions

All of us who deal with ADHD, in our families or in ourselves, can bear witness to the psychological havoc the illness can cause. Like a leaky faucet, moreover, that havoc—the unsettledness and uncertainty—can leak over and flood our spiritual lives. At times we feel awash in some foreign ebb and flow that has ripped us from our spiritual moorings.

Actually, what occurs here is not one isolated event. A grouping of events can gather together to make one feel, like David, distant from God or as if God doesn't care. Sometimes we get very uncomfortable talking about our feeling of distance from God. We believe that we are not good enough Christians, or that we're letting others down by not being strong enough, or that we're letting God down.

To find and keep our spiritual footing, we have to start at the beginning with an honest appraisal. No one is a "good enough" Christian. We are redeemed. As redeemed sons and daughters of God, we are loved for *who we are*, not just for *what we do*. We remember that "every good and perfect gift is from above, coming down from the Father of the heavenly lights, who does not change like shifting shadows" (Jas 1:17).

Being "strong enough" is relative. Our strength lies elsewhere: "This is the word of the Lord to Zerubbabel: 'Not by might nor by power, but by my Spirit,' says the Lord Almighty" (Zec 4:6). Our comfort is to turn to one who has almighty power.

"Letting God down" occurs only when we despair of his ability to help us. Mind, this is *not* the same as feeling forsaken or abandoned by God, as David did in Psalm 22. It's denying God's power altogether. It's believing that only by *my* strength, *my* actions, can I resolve this situation. It is, if you will, stripping God from his throne of majesty and power.

Yet, we wonder. ADHD bashes the fragile boats of our lives when we long for quiet waters. We tire of battling upstream at the rapids, where we feel constantly pressed backward. We want the quiet pools where we can let the boat drift under a golden sun. How do we get there? Frankly, we might never experience it fully; we understand the reality of living with ADHD. But certain understandings and actions can remind us of David's words: "Taste and see that the Lord is good; blessed is the man who takes refuge in him" (Ps 34:8). We can arrive at that understanding by considering several practical solutions and also several applicable biblical principles.

Spiritual Patterns

We discussed earlier how ADHD disrupts routines—like a cherry bomb exploding at a picnic. Since ADHD destroys routines, it is necessary to break the day into manageable segments over which we can exert some control. We try to create patterns—having dinner at relatively the same time, deliberately finding diversionary time for hobbies and reading, breaking up time with physical activities. We try to avoid long meetings; we try to break work (our own or homework for our children) into manageable segments.

Within that pattern we also have to include space reserved for devotions, prayer, and meditations. Shape it as a regular time, a routine, if you will, that can't be violated. I have personally found that I can't have my own devotional time at the end of the day. My mind is bouncing all over like a Ping-Pong ball. I'm waiting for the ball to wear out so I can go to bed. I'm better off reading the paper or a book.

Consequently, I have devotions first thing in the morning. My morning routine might seem ludicrous to some. I'm usually up first, so I let the dog out, start the coffee, then let the dog back in. After I've done ten minutes of calisthenics, the coffee is ready. And I'm ready for devotions.

Of course I experience that monster of ADHD *during* devotions, that is, distractions or inability to focus. A couple of things help me. I read Scripture or a devotional book with a pen in hand, writing in the margins. That way I "own" the passages; I enter into them, and they enter into me. Second, I keep a prayer list. If I tell someone I'll pray for them, I tell them I'd like to pray for them for the next seven days. A week gives me a workable time frame. If I leave the time frame indeterminate, I'll soon forget and start feeling guilty.

The key thing here is that it becomes a regular part of my time. I can't wait until "I feel like it." ADHD doesn't much care about "feelings." It has to be managed. So too in spiritual matters.

Affirmation

ADHD is a biochemical disorder centered in the brain. Nonetheless, it has psychological effects upon how we view ourselves, our relations with others, and our relation with God.

The distinction between biochemistry and psychology is important. At its simplest level, we treat the former with pharmaceutical approaches, and we treat the latter with therapeutic approaches. Both are designed to help us function as close to normally as possible in this world.

In practice, however, the psychological side of ADHD is far more complex than that because it calls into question our own self-worth. Consequently it also calls into question our self-worth in relations with others and with God. Perhaps one of the most distressing comments a parent can hear from an ADHD child, and yet one so frequently heard, is, "Why do I do bad things? I don't want to." These are the questions that rip at the heart of a parent. As we discussed earlier, the proper response is, "You may have done something wrong, but that doesn't mean you're a bad person. You are precious. God made you." It's proper because it's the truth.

The problem here is that those bad feelings about oneself don't miraculously disappear at some arbitrary age but persist into adulthood. Sometimes our most secret heart is still crying like that child, "Why am I so bad?" or "Why am I such a failure?" But we move through the patterns of the day and try to pretend the feelings away.

I have to be very frank here. There is no instant cure-all or neat five-step solution for this psychology. If anyone pretends to offer it to you, distrust the offer. Often it is a matter of a course of careful therapy with a professional knowledgeable about and well skilled in treating ADHD. With that important caution, there are, nonetheless, spiritual guidelines that come to bear.

First, recognize the source of the feelings. They are not, as some people are currently claiming, the work of satanic demons sent to persecute you. The feelings certainly do persecute us—we dare not deny *that* reality. The source of the feelings, however, is an illness. It's called ADHD. We know what it is, how it functions, and what its effects are. We know this as surely as we know that a broken leg causes excruciating pain. Here the pain arises from the illness psychologically: confusion, lack of concentration, fidgeting, restlessness, hyperactivity, and feelings of worthlessness and distance from God.

Just as we, as primary advocates for our children, have to pour affirmation into the troubled pitcher of their lives, so too we adults with ADHD have to do so for ourselves. Recognize that our psychological tendency is going to run toward words like *can't*. We feel we can't manage, can't succeed, can't be good enough.

The fact of the matter is that indeed we can't—not in our own strength. I call this adopting a different point of view. When I write a work of fiction, one of the early decisions I have to make is from what point of view to tell the story. Will it be first person, that is, through the eyes and mind of a character *inside* the story? Or will it be objective, told by someone (a narrator) outside the story who sees the big picture all the time? ADHD makes us see the picture too small. We have to broaden our perspective.

What we have to see with the broadening perspective is grace.

How we long to remove despair and suffering from our

lives. We cannot, of course. No amount of money, energy, or talent can buy that. But we can remind ourselves—daily—that we don't walk alone in our troubled world. Our affirmation lies not in who we think we are but in what God thinks we are. Victorious Christian living lies not in eliminating all of our problems; it is our faith in God at work in our lives during problems.

And what is that precisely? Scripture couldn't be clearer. In Matthew 23:37 Jesus cries out to Jerusalem (the people of God), "How often I have longed to gather your children together, as a hen gathers her chicks under her wings." The image here is one of comfort and protection, but it dives even more deeply into the profundity of love. We are precious to the Lord of heaven and earth. The image of the extended wings became real one Friday when Jesus extended his arms on the cross. There, in the darkness and suffering, he gathered us into his eternal life.

Into our despair shines that powerful affirmation. Look how precious you are to me! I extend my arms to gather you in and comfort you. These were the words *enacted* on the cross.

God as Coach

That heading seems trite, and I hardly dare use it. We've talked often in this book about having a coach to help plan daily and weekly affairs. If we can see God as the centering point for all those affairs, then the heading is accurate.

I am thinking here of the story of Katherine G. Bond, who told her story in *Today's Christian Woman*.[1] She discovered her disorder in a way that is increasingly common—secondhand. You see, she was a schoolteacher. She loved her teaching, but the management of all the secondary details—the grading, the lesson plans, the reports—seemed to swirl together into an insurmountable mountain. She always seemed to start too late, the mountain got higher, and nearly all-night labor seemed to cut only little chunks out of it. It wasn't until she heard a speaker on ADHD at a faculty meeting, she wrote, that she was alerted to her own disorder.

Since she was at a period of her life when she always seemed to be either pregnant or breast-feeding, she needed to take steps other than a pharmaceutical regimen. She needed new strategies for management in order to start over. As much as she loved teaching, she decided to leave the classroom that year and become a stay-at-home mom. There, she writes, "I've learned ... there are physiological factors I can control. Out of necessity, I've developed coping strategies."[2]

Several of these seem elementary but are often disregarded by adults with ADHD. For example, Bond pays attention to her physical health with a triad of basic questions: Have I eaten (nutrition)? Did I get enough sleep? Do I need to exercise? Other activities, like devotions and journaling, are carefully included in her schedule. "During this time," Bond wrote, "God often reveals strategies to help manage my day."[3]

Still, that doesn't insure a stable course. Bond's concluding statement to her activities indicates the source of her stability:

On the days when the laundry's a foothill to the Cascades, the toys have reproduced all over the living room, the dishes are hosting living organisms, and I'm late for a meeting with my child's teacher, I send up a distress signal to God. I could easily spend most of my time feeling guilty about what I've left unfinished and anxious about what I have yet to begin. But I'm learning this guilt isn't from God. He loves me as I am—and his grace makes change possible. Although the term Attention Deficit Disorder sometimes causes me to squirm, I've decided that having ADD need not be a liability in my life. In fact, my creativity and periods of intense attentiveness have allowed me to do things I might not have done otherwise, such as professional storytelling. With structure and God's grace, I'm making peace with ADD.[4]

The Dialogue With God

Many of us find ourselves incapable of the energetic act of frank and honest dialogue with God. I find two factors contributing to this.

The first is the formal quality of worship at many of our mainstream churches. Worship, or meeting God, is a serious and patterned affair. Except for "moments of silent prayer," we are *led through* worship. Correctly so, in many respects, for we are encouraged to meet together as "God's people," to be spiritually nurtured by preaching from Scripture, and to share in the communal body of Christ by the sacraments. The problem is that the formality of worship life often permeates our personal devotional and spiritual life. Out of church and its forms that feed us, we often feel distant from God and spiritually malnourished on our own.

The second contributing factor to our failure to engage in honest dialogue with God is the feeling that God doesn't want us to show our "real" emotions. Somehow it feels a bit unseemly to reveal our deepest feelings. After all, aren't we called to be "joyful Christians," million-watt smiles always in place?

Consider this example of a large group Bible study for women. It started with a fifty-minute lecture to the two to three hundred women gathered together. Then they broke into groups of ten or twelve, each with a study leader, for intensive study of the passage and a time for personal sharing of prayer needs.

In that small group intimacy, one woman, who was just recovering from a prolonged and severe postpartum depression, expressed her anger at God for the traumatic suffering of that illness. It had come about through a natural process, not through anything she had done "wrong." Hospitalized for six weeks, she hadn't been able to care for the baby the way she wished. At the time it had devastated her sense of self-worth and her ability to practice "normal" routines. When she voiced her most honest emotions, how sometimes she felt angry with God for allowing it all to happen, the study leader turned to her and said, "*Tsk, tsk, tsk.* We may never be angry with God."

May we not? I suspect that's news to God, for Scripture shows an altogether different pattern. I understand the study leader's concern—that is, we are to honor and respect God above all things. But we also walk in a personal relationship with this God we honor. We are liberated to bring all our needs—and feelings—before him. If God hadn't wanted us to use our emotions, why did he create us with them? To probe this important issue, consider one clear expression of emotional outpouring in the Bible. Only one among hundreds, it is King David's lamentation in Psalm 22.

Look at the circumstances. David had been anointed as God's king, his ambassador on earth. Yet his reign is beset by enemies on every side. Nothing seems to be going right. Dozens of new demands arise every hour of the day. Challenges defy his control. Enemies do their best to find him out, even to destroy him. No wonder the psalm begins in mourning: "My God, my God, why have you forsaken me?" The words ring down through the centuries with familiarity. Our own demands, challenges, and enemies set our schedules spinning and our minds stumbling. But we most often remember these words of David as also being the words of Jesus, God himself, from the cross. Jesus shared the very same emotions as the woebegone David.

These words of rejection and lostness are just the beginning of David's heartfelt dialogue with God. He wonders why God, with all his power, doesn't just step in and change things (vv. 1-2). The psalm does not languish in despair, however, for in verse three David affirms his faith and trust in God *even in adversity*. Because of his faith and trust he dares speak his inmost thoughts.

His plea changes from intercession by God to change things now to a plea to keep him close to God: "Do not be far from me, for trouble is near and there is no one to help" (v. 11). David is afraid. His heart "melts like wax" (v. 14). He pours these feelings out before God knowing he needs help beyond his own resources.

Here a curious thing happens. As David reflects on his state, it is almost as if the Great Deliverer enters *into* his state.

Indeed, that is precisely what happened historically. Notice that David's self-descriptive imagery precisely matches Jesus' crucifixion imagery. "My strength is dried up like a potsherd, and my tongue sticks to the roof of my mouth" (v. 15). We remember Jesus so weakened by sleeplessness and torment that he couldn't bear his own cross. We remember Jesus crying from the cross, "I thirst."

The imagery continues, matching the reality of Jesus at every step: "A band of evil men has encircled me, they have pierced my hands and my feet" (v. 16). "They divide my garments among them and cast lots for my clothing" (v. 18). This is the cry of a man tormented beyond understanding; only the deepest need pours out.

So too it often is in the furious swirl of our lives. But just as these passages, read in the full scope of the Bible, indicate that God is near to David, so too we can know that on this side of the crucifixion we are with Jesus. David's triumphant knowledge is ours as well: "He has not despised or disdained the suffering of the afflicted one; he has not hidden his face from him but has listened to his cry for help" (v. 24).

The Dialogue Answered

When we speak our anger, anxiety, fear, or bewilderment unto God, we are not met with indifferent silence. That, by the way, is the belief of the postmodern world at large. Since we are alone in a world of mere matter, the postmodernist has it, we have only ourselves to rely upon. David didn't hold that belief for a second. Nor should we.

Where do we hear God's answer? Sometimes it may come,

as Katherine Bond suggests, in a direct way during devotions or journaling. Sometimes it may come through friends or relatives who speak God's peace in our ears. But always and unfailingly it comes from God himself in his Word.

I often like to read the Old Testament prophets. They seem to me epitomes of courage and truth, ready to put their lives on the line to speak for God. Here's Nathan chastising David. Or Elijah facing down Ahab and mocking Baal. Daniel peers down the centuries and sees a vision of last things eerily similar to what John saw on Patmos hundreds of years later. Or Isaiah, speaking words of God's peace during a time of spiritual aridity, when the people seemed no longer to want to talk with or hear from God.

Isaiah, perhaps, provided the ultimate prophecy of our peace. In Isaiah 9 we find God's promise of the Messiah to fulfill his answers to us. But Isaiah also conveys God's peace in our *present* circumstance. These words in Isaiah 43 are spoken to us here and now, as responses to our dialogue with God:

> But now, this is what the Lord says—
> he who created you, O Jacob,
> he who formed you, O Israel:
> "Fear not, for I have redeemed you;
> I have summoned you by name; you are mine.
> When you pass through the waters,
> I will be with you;
> and when you pass through the rivers,
> they will not sweep over you.
> When you walk through the fire,
> you will not be burned;

the flames will not set you ablaze.
For I am the Lord, your God,
the Holy One of Israel, your Savior.

ISAIAH 43:1-3

The entire chapter is a testimony to God's graciousness and goodness. His power will sustain when it seems all our power is spent. When it seems we are sucked to and fro in crashing waters, he will lift us. When the flames of demands torch our lives, he will drape his protection about us.

We don't raise our bewildered lamentation to a silent heaven. The answer lies right before us as we open the pages of God's Book and read his letter to us.

The Precious Stone

Since childhood years I have loved to travel to northern Michigan.

Nearly every summer my father would pack the six of us in the old turtle-back Ford and we would be off to the land of adventure. We didn't travel fast, and we didn't make many plans. Mother would be in the front seat with a map and from time to time exclaim, "Oh, that sounds interesting. Let's go there." And so we did. That was our itinerary and guidebook.

In the old photo albums I have the black-and-white testimonials. There we are standing before Pipagwa's Wigwam in St. Croix. Stoic-faced Ojibwa Indians in oiled deerskins sold trinkets we couldn't afford but carried home in our minds like wonders of a lost world—arrowheads, knives in leather sheaths, deerskin-clad dolls with braided black hair. And here we are atop a dune at the lakeshore. In the photo Grandma stands by the old Ford looking up at us. And here my older sister and I are at the shore collecting stones in old tin coffee cans.

To recall those many trips when I was young, I once took my own family camping far into the northern peninsula, heading north until we stopped at the last little jut of land into Lake Superior—as far north as we could go. I retraced memories. My family beheld new wonders.

More often, however, we take a short camping or motel trip up to one of the small towns along the Lake Michigan shore-line—Petosky, Traverse City, Charlevoix, Harbor Springs. If you visit Traverse City, you can turn northwest and follow the west bay through rolling groves of cherry trees. Their petals in spring are like colorful clouds caught in black branches.

We drive past the old fishing village of Northport and on along roads you wouldn't know were there unless someone had given you directions. Fortunately we have directions. Long-time friends have a summer home in the area and long ago gave us a key to use it as we wished.

The shoreline along the west bay has no sandy beaches. One has to drive across to the Lake Michigan side for that. Nonetheless, it is one of the most fascinating shorelines I have ever walked. It's really a large treasure box that invites you in for a treasure hunt.

Here's the way we hunt. We wear old sneakers, for one thing. Remember we're walking on stones, some broken and jagged. Sometimes the old tennis shoes will come out lacerated. We walk in water about six inches deep. That way we can pick out the stones that the waves wash over on the shore side and also those in slightly deeper water.

We are looking for Petosky stones. When they lie under-water, these prehistoric fossils glitter with intricate patterns, as beguiling as a new puzzle. When dry they seem like any common, grayish stone. One wouldn't give them a second glance.

Others who know where and how to look may take them home and polish them to a lustrous glow with rock polishers or by the hand method of fine sandpaper and jeweler's rouge. We have bags of unpolished stones in the garage. Some of the nicer ones I dump in the fish tank, a few I've polished the easy way, with a coat of polyurethane, and kept in my office. They are reminders, not only of the travels we have made but of the beauty that can lie under a dusty skin. I've often seen people in my office almost automatically reach out to one of the stones, admire its beauty, peer closely at its multiple variegations of fossil imprints, turn its smooth surface over in searching fingers.

Inevitably if they are not Michigan natives, they wonder about the stone's origin. For such people there are certain lessons about the Petosky stone. First one has to know what they are. The fossil imprints occurred at some point beyond our counting when God caused the great glaciers to shift and scour the bedrock. Then one has to know where to find them. One has to go toward them to receive their gift, to discover their beauty under the dusty skin. Then too, one has to know their intrinsic worth. Truly, tourist shops by the dozens in the Michigan coastal towns sell the highly polished stones. They arrive from the polishing drums looking like buffed jewels.

But a Petosky stone is not simply a bauble to behold, like a piece of costume jewelry. It holds an inner, only partially revealed, beauty. One really comes to treasure it by, say, dipping a wet finger on it, watching the shapes mysteriously come to life with a profound beauty. One should also be aware of its enduring beauty. Like diamonds locked as carbon deposits deep in the earth, Petosky stones wash mysteriously from the depths and storms of Lake Michigan. When you hold one, you get the feeling that something incredibly old, beyond time's reckoning, is present here and now. It is very nearly a feeling of awe.

Interestingly, God, who made these Petosky stones, often reveals himself or his special relationship with humanity through stones. For example, when God called Moses to the mountaintop to reveal his direct will for human living, the message was inscribed on Moses' tablets of stone. A cynic might observe that of course they had to be. Moses didn't carry around a Cross pen and a legal pad. The effect doesn't change, however. Here the enduring and beautiful promises of God are inscribed on stone. Similarly, God revealed his faithful mercy when he ordered Moses to strike the rock at Horeb and sweet water flowed out of it. Here the stone provided physical nourishment and, in the searing desert, life itself.

As one turns to the more prophetic books of the Old Testament, however, the references to stones take on a more expectant, urgent, and searching tone. It is almost as if we are wading the lakeshore, looking for that one Petosky stone couched among so many common rocks.

Some of the same lessons, in fact, also seem to apply as we search out the cornerstone of our faith—the living presence of Jesus himself. We no longer seek out "what they are" but who he is. Jesus is the living stone, into whom we are mortared for our spiritual life. We find him not among the shops and splendors of this life but revealed in God's Word and in our very lives. We find Jesus in a relationship.

As such, this precious cornerstone bears intrinsic worth, that is, he alone is the source of our spiritual relationship. As God released the sweet water from the rock at Horeb, so he releases the living water to us through Jesus. No striking of the rock occurred; instead, the whips striped the flesh that, as Isaiah wrote, bore our grief and "carried our sorrows" (53:4).

Above all, this rock Jesus bears enduring beauty. Surely he was bruised and disfigured in *this* life like a dusty gray Petosky stone lying on dry shore. Few imagined the beauty he carried. But then we realize that Jesus is not, indeed, some prehistoric fossil but a living presence at this moment, at this place. He is not time-bound in any sense. Jesus is eternal God, who saw fit to enter our time briefly to do his mighty work of eternal salvation.

Here is the mystery, and the consummate beauty, of the One who is our cornerstone.

It is also the mystery of our intrinsic worth as children of God. Our faith is marked not only by what we do but also by what we believe. Our lives may often seem discolored, dusky, and gray. Disorders such as ADHD seem to rock our firm foundations. But not if we stand on the precious cornerstone. "I have redeemed you. I have called you by name. You are mine."

I lift the Petosky stone off the shelf, feel its smooth contours under my fingers. I touch its surface with moisture and watch the mysterious whorls appear. It almost seems that the stone reaches back with its inner life. Beauty beyond the superficial, beauty beyond comprehension. So too the beauty in each life God has given.

Appendix A: The Ritalin Controversy

If you are the parents of an ADHD child, you've heard all the cautionary statements and questions: "Ritalin makes a child wired." "Ritalin is dangerous to a child." "What lingering effects can it have?" "Is Ritalin addictive?"

These common concerns intensified when Dr. Peter Breggin launched a full frontal assault upon Ritalin in an article for *The Journal of College Student Psychotherapy* (1995)[1]. Breggin argued that the behavior of children showing ADHD symptoms is usually triggered by outside stressors rather than internal disorders. His view of children is largely grounded in behavioralism and humanitarian idealism: "When treated with respect, they tend to respond respectfully. When loved, they tend to be loving."[2] Surely all children deserve respect and love, but are these sufficient for managing ADHD disorders?

Breggin advocates a program he calls Dad Attention Deficit Disorder (DADD). "In my clinical experience," he writes, "most so-called ADHD children are not receiving sufficient attention from their fathers who are separated from the family, too preoccupied with work and other things, or otherwise impaired in their ability to parent."[3] Blame it on good old Dad. The corrective, then, is for fathers to spend a great deal more quality time with their children.

Just as with the concepts of respect and love, so too we find here a kernel of truth. Of course it is important for fathers to spend quality, individual time with their children. But is that sufficient to deal with ADHD, even "so-called" ADHD? And just how much time is required? What tasks does Dad give up?

Breggin overtly claims that "ADHD is not a disorder but a manifestation of conflict," with no apparent biological cause. Consequently he thoroughly discredits the use of Ritalin, which has a biochemical effect. He calls it "toxic psychiatry."

Stimulated by Breggin's views, the law firm of Walters and Kraus, L.L.P., filed a class action in Texas against the manufacturers of Ritalin, against CHADD (because they have received donations from the manufacturer, Ciba/Novartis), and against the American Psychiatric Association. Dr. Breggin is the law firm's medical consultant.

In general, the suit alleges "fraud and conspiracy." In particular, "Ciba/Novartis planned, conspired, and colluded to create, develop, and promote the diagnosis of Attention Deficit Disorder (ADD) and Attention Deficit Hyperactivity Disorder (ADHD) in a highly successful effort to increase the market for its product Ritalin." The suit then lists (extensively) possible side effects of Ritalin and an invitation to join the class-action filing.

If one combines the dire warnings of Dr. Breggin and the lawsuit, the effect is sufficient to drive anyone into anxiety over the use of Ritalin. These are not simply the precautionary warnings a medical doctor routinely gives about a medication. These statements indicate that we are poisoning and damaging ourselves and our children for *no clear need.*

In addition to Dr. Breggin's claim that there is no biochemical basis for ADHD, or that there is virtually no such illness, and the legal attacks upon Ciba/Novartis to discredit Ritalin, a third element enters the fray. Many people, including many whom we would assume to be knowledgeable about such disorders, still remain woefully ignorant about them. In *It's Nobody's Fault,* Dr. Koplewicz relates one such example:

One worried mother called me because the principal at her child's school said her son shouldn't be taking the Ritalin I had prescribed (and to which he was responding wonderfully well). The Ritalin is a crutch, the principal said; what the child really needed was a lighter school schedule and a different teacher. I was shocked by the principal's ignorance, not to mention his colossal nerve. If I had prescribed two puffs of an inhaler to keep a child with asthma from wheezing during gym class, I doubt that the principal would have suggested that the child forget the medicine and be excused from gym instead.[4]

Dr. Koplewicz adds that "when children are on medication, it's not just the parents who are judged. Teachers and others sometimes look askance at the children themselves."[5] While the stigma is certainly lessening today, the occasional negative commentary can in itself lead parents to question the use of Ritalin.

These views were partially countered by a statement in the April 8, 1998, issue of *The Journal of the American Medical Association* (*JAMA*). Based on a study spanning the years 1975 to 1997, researchers found "little evidence of widespread overdiagnosis or misdiagnosis of ADHD, or of widespread overprescription of methyl phenidate [Ritalin]." That only answers part of the equation. Is Ritalin a safe alternative for treating ADHD, if we assume, unlike Dr. Breggin, that there is indeed such a biochemical disorder?

Unlike Dr. Breggin's radical opposition to Ritalin, recent years have also seen a marked increase in homeopathic or alternative treatments that don't necessarily condemn Ritalin altogether. A number of these, for example, focus on diet plans. It has been clearly demonstrated that ADHD is not caused by diet (use of sugar, for example), but these plans suggest organic means to alleviate the symptoms. Other programs focus intensively upon cognitive learning skills and behavioral management. Yet we are left with the question, is the first-line defense of stimulant medication safe and effective?

The answer of the vast majority of psychiatrists is yes. An unqualified yes. Ritalin does have some side effects, as do all psychotropic drugs. Loss of appetite, loss of sleep, and elevated heart rate are the three most common to Ritalin, and these may be temporary or enduring. In my own case I have decided that the life I am able to live with the medications for ADHD and bipolar disorder is inestimably better, even with the side effects, than the pure chaos I have experienced without them.

Beyond that, however, the professional estimation of Ritalin is clear. Here are Doctors Hallowell and Ratey in *Driven to Distraction*:

> A few things the stimulants do *not* do should be mentioned to clear up common misconceptions. They do not "drug up" or cloud the sensorium of the individual taking them. They are not addictive in the doses prescribed for ADD. They do not take away the creativity or "special something" so many people with ADD possess.[6]

One important qualification clearly emerges, however. Ritalin is not an instant cure-all for ADHD. It helps control certain biochemical processes in the brain, most notably dopamine flow, and thus enables the person to focus better and to be less restless and less impulsive. But a parent cannot just give Ritalin and expect to walk away from the task.

In his book *The Hyperactive Child* Christian psychologist Grant Martin ably outlines strategies for dealing with the behaviors of ADHD. Martin sees medication and training as necessarily concurrent for the well-being of the child:

> The most important concept to emerge from the vast amounts of research about ADHD is that no treatment approach is successful alone. Neither medical, behavioral, psychological, nor educational intervention is adequate by itself. We must be conscious of treating the *whole* child or adolescent. Successful intervention makes a difference both on the short term and on the long term. We want to make changes which will help bring about the necessary confidence, competence, organization, discipline, and character in your child. But we also want changes that will last a lifetime.[7]

Even assuming these things about stimulant treatment, however, we as parents of children with ADHD (or we ourselves) often wonder whether we are doing the right thing by introducing a stimulant into our child's daily regimen. Ultimately the issue focuses on this question: Does the child have a fuller and more peaceful life with the medication or without? And then ask yourself the same question as a parent.

In my personal experience with ADHD, my other, complicating factor of bipolar disorder involves a far more complex regimen of medication. I take Ritalin only on an "as needed" basis, since the other medications affect ADHD secondarily. I have learned to be content with it. At the beginning of this study I stressed that I have an illness, *but I am not the illness that I have.* Without the use of proper medication and careful monitoring of it, I would not be able to make that claim. In this case the medicine has allowed me to be the person God made me to be.

Appendix B: Helpful Resources for ADHD

Children and Adults with Attention-Deficit/Hyperactivity Disorders (CHADD)
8181 Professional Place, Suite 201
Landover, MD 20785
301-306-7070 and fax 301-306-7090
800-233-4050
Web site: http://www.chadd.org/

Learning Disabilities Association of America
4156 Library Road
Pittsburgh, PA 15234
412-341-1515 and fax 412-344-0224
Web site: http://www.ldanatl.org

National Attention Deficit Disorder Association (ADDA)
1788 Second Street, Suite 200
Highland Park, IL 60035
847-432-ADDA and fax 847-432-5874
Web site: http://www.add.org

National Center for Learning Disabilities
381 Park Avenue South, Suite 1401
New York, NY 10016
212-545-7510 and fax 212-545-9665
888-575-7373
Web site: http://www.ncld.org

Additional Web Sites
The American Medical Association: http://www.ama-assn.org
National Mental Health Association: http://www.nmha.org
National Institutes of Health: http://www.nih.gov
Health Center: http://www2.health-center.com

Notes

TWO

1. *Diagnostic and Statistical Manual of Mental Disorders, Third Edition* (Washington, D.C.: The American Psychiatric Association, 1980). Also known as the *DSM-III.*
2. *Diagnostic and Statistical Manual of Mental Disorders, Fourth Edition-Text Revision* (Washington, D.C.: The American Psychiatric Association, 2000). Also known as the *DSM-IV.*
3. All details taken from the *Physicians' Desk Reference,* also known as the *PDR* (Montvale, N.J.: Medical Economics Co., 1998).

THREE

1. Edward Hallowell, M.D., and John Ratey, M.D., *Driven to Distraction* (New York: Simon and Schuster, 1994). See also their sequel, *Answers to Distraction* (New York: Bantam, 1996).
2. Hallowell and Ratey, *Driven to Distraction,* 42.
3. *DSM-IV,* 92-93.

FOUR

1. Harold Koplewicz, M.D., *It's Nobody's Fault* (New York: Random House, 1996).
2. Koplewicz, xii.

FIVE

1. A helpful resource for dealing with ADHD situations at school is G.J. DuPaul and G. Stoner, *ADHD in the Schools: Assessment and Intervention Strategies* (New York: Guilford, 1994).
2. For further information, see Joseph Biederman, "Attention-Deficit/Hyperactivity Disorder: A Life-Span Perspective," *Journal of Clinical Psychiatry* 59 (Supplement 7): 4-16; and S.R. Pliszka, "Comorbidity of Attention-Deficit/Hyperactivity Disorder with Psychiatric Disorder," *Journal of Clinical Psychiatry* 59 (Supplement 7): 50-55B.
3. *CHADD Fact Sheets: AD/HD and Co-Existing Disorders.* www.chadd.org.
4. "Ritalin: Mom's Little Helper," *Time*, February 12, 2001, 73.
5. J.J. Rucklidge and B.J. Kaplan, "Psychological Functioning of Women Identified in Adulthood with Attention-Deficit/Hyperactivity Disorder," *Journal of Attention Disorders* 2 (1997): 167-76.

SIX

1. T.W. Phelan, *One-Two-Three-Magic: Training Your Child to Do What You Want* (Glen Ellyn, Ill.: Child Management, 1995).

SEVEN

1. Koplewicz, 53.

EIGHT

1. *DSM-IV*, 89.
2. *DSM-IV*, 90.
3. Kathleen Nadeau, *ADHD in the Workplace: Choices, Changes, Challenges* (Bristol, Penn.: Brunner/Mazel, 1997).
4. Gordon MacDonald, *Ordering Your Private World* (Nashville: Thomas Nelson, 1985), 41-62.

NINE

1. Katherine G. Bond, "Adult ADHD: Could You Have This Disorder?" *Today's Christian Woman* (November/December 2000), 75-77.
2. Bond, 76.
3. Bond, 77.
4. Bond, 77.

Appendix A

1. Peter R. Breggin and Ginger Ross Breggin, "The Hazards of Treating Attention-Deficit/Hyperactivity Disorder with Methyl pheridate (Ritalin)," *Journal of College Student Psychotherapy.*
2. Breggin, 59.
3. Breggin, 60.
4. Koplewicz, 59.
5. Koplewicz, 60.
6. Hallowell and Ratey, *Driven to Distraction,* 238.
7. Grant Martin, *The Hyperactive Child* (Wheaton, Ill.: Victor, 1992), 140.